SEFTON
THE STORY OF A CAVALRY HORSE

SEFTON

The Story of a Cavalry Horse

J.N.P. WATSON

With a Foreword by
The Rt. Hon. The Earl of Westmorland, K.C.V.O.
Late Royal Horse Guards (the Blues)
and Equitation Officer of the Household Cavalry
Master of the Horse to Her Majesty The Queen

SOUVENIR PRESS
London

First published 1983 by Souvenir Press Ltd,
43 Great Russell Street, London WC1B 3PA
and simultaneously in Canada

ISBN 0 285 62587 X casebound
ISBN 0 285 62602 7 paperback

Photoset and printed in Great Britain by
Redwood Burn Limited, Trowbridge, Wiltshire

Foreword

I am very pleased to have been invited to write a short foreword to this book. John Watson and I were in the Blues together and both of us had the privilege of serving with the Mounted Squadrons at Knightsbridge Barracks.

I am sure that everyone was horrified by the act of violence that took place in Hyde Park on the 20th July, 1982, when four members of the Guard and seven horses were killed while carrying out purely ceremonial duties. For me this occasion was the more shattering because I myself had ridden so many times on Queen's Guard; I am glad that I have been able to play a small part in the campaign for a memorial to be erected in Hyde Park, to ensure that the public, and past and present members of the Household Cavalry, will never forget that dreadful day.

It seems ironic that for many years Sefton was considered unsuitable as a ceremonial troop horse. He was one of the oldest horses on Parade that day and suffered appalling wounds when the nail bomb was detonated. Taken back to Knightsbridge, he was cared for with all the skill and kindness possible.

The one thing that Sefton did not lack was courage. He had proved this many times in his early years with the Regiment when he had become a successful cross country horse, and there is no doubt that this courage enabled him slowly to recover from his dreadful injuries. The interest and affection which have been shown to Sefton are recorded in this charming and beautifully illustrated book, and I am sure that it will be much appreciated by the public and in the Regiment.

The Earl of Westmorland, KCVO
Master of the Horse

This book is dedicated to All Ranks of
the Household Cavalry at home and abroad

ACKNOWLEDGEMENTS

My thanks are due, firstly, to Lieutenant-Colonel A.H. Parker Bowles, Blues and Royals (Commanding the Household Cavalry Mounted Regiment, 1980–83), who read my typescripts with the greatest care, and without whose support and encouragement the book would scarcely have been possible. And, next, to Major C. N. Haworth-Booth (late The Life Guards) who first put forward the idea of a book about Sefton, and who supplied me with much information about the horse's career in Germany.

Also to Lieutenant-Colonel and Riding Master A. Jackson, commanding the Mounted Regiment's Equitation Wing, and his Warrant Officer, Corporal-Major D. McGregor, who trained Sefton; Veterinary-Major N.H. Carding and his assistant, Farrier-Major B. Smith; Colonel K.R. Morgan-Jones, Royal Army Veterinary Corps, and his Adjutant, Major P.A. Roffey; Corporal Islay Forbes, Women's Royal Army Corps, who had charge of Sefton during his 1982 convalescence; Major S.V. Gilbart-Denham (The Life Guards) of Headquarters Paderborn Garrison, BAOR; Major J. Mc M. Carr-Ellison, Captain B.W.B. White-Spunner and Trooper M. Pedersen, all of the Blues and Royals Mounted Squadron; Mr R. Batey (late The Life Guards); Mr C.W. Frearson, of the Household Cavalry Museum; Major W.T.V. Loyd (late The Life Guards); Major H.W. Schofield (late Royal Army Pay Corps) of the *Guards Magazine* and his assistant, Mrs E. McNab.

To Miss Christine Bousfield, Miss Elizabeth Lloyd and Mr John King for permission to reproduce their paintings; to Mrs Richard Wilkinson, who supplied me with photographs of her late husband riding Sefton; Mr Michael Connors, the dealer who sold Sefton to the Army; Mr John Stevens, Director of the Horse of the Year Show; the Editors of the *Guards Magazine* and the *Daily Star* for allowing me to quote from their publications; and to my wife, Lavinia, who typed the manuscript and all the correspondence connected with the book.

Pannett's Shipley, J.N.P.W.
Horsham,
Sussex.

Contents

Foreword 5
Acknowledgements 6
Preface 9
1 Irish Born and Bred 11
2 In the Hands of Trooper McGregor 19
3 How to Disgrace the Queen's Birthday Parade 28
4 On Queen's Life Guard, then Failed Again 33
5 Instructing the Recruits 40
6 A Blues and Royals Horse 45
7 The Joys of Camping 48
8 Proclaimed 'King' in Germany 55
9 Glamorous Knightsbridge 66
10 Royal Occasions *Par Excellence* 73
11 The Fateful Morning 80
12 The Horse of the Year 95
Epilogue 105
Index 112

Preface

Some weeks after I handed in the text and pictures for this book, a television journalist, reacting to advance publicity, telephoned me to enquire why there was so much hullabaloo about a mere horse? Why was our pity reserved for the animals? Why no book about the cavalrymen? If Sefton warranted a biography, why not one or more of the wounded men, too? How could the life of a horse be more important than that of a man?

I reminded him of how the British public had responded to those atrocities in London in July, 1982, how its compassion had gone out largely to the horses, to the soldiers only second. But why? The explanation can be found partly in the 'dumb creature' syndrome. When animals, who are without sin, are the victims of men's cruelty, there is a collective sorrow, a tenderness of a special brand, a sense of shame and a passion for revenge, just as there is when babies or children suffer from savagery or neglect. The soldiers had incurred the hatred of the IRA by being soldiers. The horses, said the sympathisers, were not carrying the soldiers from choice. By any standards they were as innocent as new-born babes.

There was also, in this case, perhaps, an element of the concept – mistaken or accurately intuitive, according to personal opinion – that the larger the wounded or maimed animal the greater the volume and degree of pain; and that, because horses do not scream in agony, do not yelp like dogs or howl like cats when they are hurt, they have little outlet for their feelings. So, all the more must we humans weep for them. Many of those mourners would say that animals are more deserving of our sympathy than injured human beings, who automatically receive comfort from family, friends and hospital staffs. Anyhow, those who were not deeply moved by the sight, on their television sets, of the wounded beasts bleeding on the South Carriageway that July morning, some kneeling, bewildered, others prostrate, attempting to raise their heads with anguish and terror in their eyes, can hardly call themselves true animal-lovers.

There are a great many horses all over the world that are treated vilely by mankind, whether with wanton cruelty or neglect: draft horses and riding school horses, racehorses and military horses, pack horses, competition horses and horses going for meat on the hoof. A host of owners and exploiters have a great deal to answer for. In contrast, this book is about a horse that has become a great exemplar of all those equines that have been given wonderfully happy and productive lives. For no horse that is foaled

Corporal Islay Forbes poses with Sefton. (Daily Express)

today could have the promise of a more contented future than one that is destined for the British Army.

But, as the troop horses are nothing without their trainers and riders, the reader will soon find that this is a tribute to the soldiers at Hyde Park Barracks, too. It is about the centaur-like co-ordination of horse and trooper, about joy derived from man-and-animal healthy living, mutual discipline and high endeavour. It is a story of the unparalleled magnificence of pageantry that, in the Household Cavalry, emerges from those combinations. Since Britain's beloved Sefton has come to be regarded, not only as the embodiment of equine nobility and the equine virtues, but also, in a way, as a manifestation and a symbol of all the Household Cavalry stands for, surely there could be no more cogent or lasting memorial to the cavaliers who suffered on that awful morning than an account of his life and the men who made him what he is.

J.N.P.W.

1 Irish Born and Bred

This is the story of a Household Cavalry horse, a horse who was foaled in 1963 and who first changed hands in 1964, yet whose pedigree is unknown. More than 90 per cent of the horses earmarked for the Household Cavalry were bred in Ireland. Most were by thoroughbred stallions, leased from the Irish Department of Agriculture, out of draught mares or hunters belonging to farmers or small breeders. The majority were produced in the south of the country, where a lot of farm work was done by draught horse. The horse of this story probably came from such a dam, but she may have been of finer quality, perhaps a threequarters bred hunter. We do not know.

Since the young horse with which we are concerned possessed neither name nor number for the first four years of his life, you will know him for the time being as Horse of Destiny, for one day his name would ring round the world.

His breeder would have weaned him when he was six months old. After that he would have brought him in at night and fed him on oats and bran and beet pulp. At that stage, too, he would have gelded him, for few purchasers, nowadays, want entires, except in the case of thoroughbreds, for breeding. Entires are too strong and wild and intractable, and if they have access to mares, they embarrass the breeding system. Yet, as we shall see, Horse of Destiny remained very much a male, with a male personality and male instincts.

Although we are not aware who bred him, we do know who bought him from his breeder and sold him to the British Army. It was Mr Michael Connors, the most prominent of the dealers then trading in horses for the British Army. The horses in question were wanted by the Household Cavalry, the King's Troop of the Royal Horse Artillery and, to a much lesser extent, the Royal Army Veterinary Corps (for the Army School of Equitation); by the Royal Corps of Transport (to train men in horsemastership for their Hong Kong Pack Transport Company*); by the mounted element of the Royal Corps of Military Police†, and, for ceremonial purposes, by senior officers of the Foot Guards.

The Army were just as particular in selecting their horses in 1967, when Horse of Destiny went to them, as they are now. Take the Horse Gunners. Although, so far as colour was concerned, the King's Troop did not mind whether their equine recruits were brown, bay or black, they did insist upon

* Disbanded 1975
† 167 Provost Company

'It came easily to imagine Horse of Destiny in that paradise environment 17 or 18 years before.' (Richard Earle)

'good quality hunter' types that could gallop briskly; and, for their gun carriages, they were looking for three distinct sizes: the 'leaders' had to measure 15.3 to 16.0 hands, the 'centres' 15.2 to 15.3 hands and the 'wheelers' 15.1 to 15.2. All the other Army horses must be over 16.0 hands, the drum horses over 17.0. The Household Cavalry colour requirements were rigid: black for officers' chargers and troop horses, grey for trumpeters and 'coloureds' for drum horses.

The wastage rate was such that the Royal Army Veterinary Corps, who were in control of purchasing remounts, were looking for an average of 50 horses a year, of which at least half were needed by the Household Cavalry. So the greatest requirement was for blacks. Nor, as Mr Connors and the other dealers would have told you, did the demand for blacks end with Britain's Household Cavalry. The Italians, who fielded a horse mountain battery, were searching for them, too, and so were the Swiss Army.

In the world of cavalry the words 'black' and 'warlike' were once synonymous. Black horses, more than any others, so it was believed, could

Mr Michael Connors with horses earmarked for sale to the British Army. Horse of Destiny lived off these fields in County Waterford until he was four years old. (The Author)

Forerunner of Horse of Destiny: a black charger carrying a soldier of the Earl of Oxford's Royal Regiment of Horse – afterwards the Royal Horse Guards (the Blues) – in the 1660s. 'In the world of cavalry, the words "black" and "warlike" were once synonymous.' (BBC Hulton Picture Library)

fill the enemy's hearts with awe. Thus when Charles II established Britain's first standing army in 1661 – with his personal bodyguard, The Life Guards, at their head – the horses were as jet as could be. As King Charles's army burgeoned, they were black for all the cavalry regiments, until the cavalry of the line – that is to say all the cavalry regiments other than the Household Cavalry – took whatever colours happened to cover suitable horses. Alternatively, regiments were granted distinguishing colours, such as greys for the 2nd Dragoons (Royal Scots Greys) and bays for the 2nd Dragoon Guards (Queen's Bays). But the Household Cavalry have always kept and jealously cherished their black 'uns.

Now Horse of Destiny possessed a white blaze and four white socks. His blaze covered most of his face, while the socks on his forelegs enveloped his fetlocks, and those of his hind legs pointed close to his hocks. He was just about as white as a black horse could be. In his case those markings may have had a significance. They seemed to symbolise the character he would soon earn, a reputation for impishness, for a wry sense of humour, coupled with showmanship and a partiality for attention. It was as though, tongue-in-cheek, Horse of Destiny knew that Her Majesty's Household Cavalry tolerated white markings, but by no means favoured them. The fewer the better. It was as though his instinct was already telling him just how far he could venture with impunity down the road of impertinence, even if he had never heard of the old adage:

One white sock, buy him!
Two white socks, try him!
Three white socks, leave him alone!
Four white socks, stay at home!

More ominous for Horse of Destiny was that other old Irish superstition:

Four white legs and a white nose,
Shoot him, skin him and give him to the crows!

He was as playful and mischievous as any purchase Mr Connors had ever made, always dancing, rearing and bucking, with a jocular catch-me-if-you-can look in his eyes – eyes which showed rather a lot of white, supposedly a bad omen in any horse. But Mr Connors, who valued unruly behaviour as a healthy sign in fillies and young geldings, reckoned he was a fine candidate for the Household Cavalry. High spirits could be channelled into useful performance.

The first lesson in the career of Horse of Destiny was to walk up the ramp of a horse box. (He was always as good as gold when it suited him). The box was driven to a property 15 miles away from Mr Connors' stud at Pallas Woodstown, to a townsland called Tullyvolahane, south-west of Waterford City, close to where the Atlantic breakers crashed against the rocks of Ireland's south coast. On that wild place of lush pasture Horse of Destiny and the two dozen others of his vintage would spend the next three years of their lives, putting on bone and sinew, maturing for the military roles that lay ahead.

No one has quite placed their finger on a central reason why Ireland –

Mr Connors by the loose boxes in County Waterford where Horse of Destiny was stabled immediately prior to his sale to the Army. (The Author)

particularly the south, the counties of Cork, Waterford, Wexford and Wicklow – is so good for horses, why the best draught horses and hunters are bred there, why famous racehorses, showjumpers and eventers are placed at stud there. Merely to exclaim that 'the grass is so wonderful!' would be to oversimplify. Perhaps the Gulf Stream climate contributes. It may be that part of the answer lies in the minerals in that soft crystal water carried through the meadows by those tinkling streams that are tributaries of such rivers as the Suir, the Bandon, the Barrow and the Blackwater. Mr Connors told me that he attributes much value to the protective nature of the big banks, which are a salient feature of the country. Then there is the human factor: the Irishman's inherent way with a horse.

When, in February, 1983, I wandered across those fields where Horse of Destiny and his contemporaries whiled away the days between 1964 and 1967, despite the foul weather the pasture shone like emeralds; the gorse, clumped around the rocky outcrops, was bright as fire below the purple backcloth of the Comeragh mountains; crystal brooks coursed through the meadowland on their way to join the Mahon river, while a dozen young horses, grazing luxuriously, bloomed in their long, woolly coats.

It came easily to imagine Horse of Destiny in that paradise environment, 17 or 18 years before, basking in the sun as, languid step by languid step, his nose, tongue and eye chose his grasses, while he swished his glossy, unkempt tail around his quarters, or twitched his ears, or brought up a hind foot to scratch against his girth, warding off the flies. It was not difficult to see, in the mind's eye, the horse that would one day trot down the Mall in full regalia – while a hundred press cameras sought him out in the ranks – rolling, in his early years, in the dusty places of those Elysian fields, of that Waterford clay, not just for sheer joy but to keep his pelt in good trim, too, to rid it of unwanted visitors. Or frolicking with his companions, or making sudden spurts across the pasture, finishing with a buck or two, suppling his limbs. Or, in winter, searching with greater intent for the more succulent herbage, or crouching with resignation under the lea of the blackthorn, against the Atlantic tempests.

His later record suggests that he would have been both more alert and more curious than most of his comrades; would have cocked his ears and pricked his nostrils towards the least noise; would always have observed the badger that came in and out of the ditch as regular as clockwork, or the old dog fox that set off across his pasture on nights when the north wind swept the golden leaf across the tussocks, or, when winter was gone, stepped lightly across the primrose banks in search of infant rabbits. He would have noticed any change in the way the starlings rose and fell like fishermen's nets on the nearby trees, he would have taken in every movement of the schoolchildren who sometimes stopped on the tarmac lane below to stare at Mr Connors' horses.

He and his fellows did not see much of man during those three years. Mr Connors visited them twice a week with some apples in his pockets, and once every two months a blacksmith would walk up and put halters on their heads and lead them down to the road to trim their feet. Cavorting with the young geldings and mares who shared his 60-acre enclosure, Horse of Destiny led an idyllic existence, a seemingly interminable heaven reserved for growing horses of potential value. And, as he filled out and put on bone, it became increasingly clear that something rather distinguished was emerging from his breeding. With such shoulders and such hocks, Mr Connors was thinking, this gelding could soon be jumping like a cat.

That April, in answer to a call for reinforcements from the British Army, Mr Connors brought the horses in from grass, and started feeding them up on oats and bran and beet pulp.

The Army Purchasing Commission, composed of Lieutenant-Colonel John Spurrey, the Commandant of the Royal Army Veterinary Corps Depot, together with a representative from the Army's London District and a veterinary officer, stayed overnight on May 31, 1967, at the Grand Hotel, Tramore. Next morning they drove to the stud at Pallas Woodstown. Mr Connors met them at his house, a low Georgian building, white, elegant, secluded, surrounded by ancient trees, cedars, chestnuts and cherries. He gave the British officers glasses of Irish coffee, well topped with cream, the regular morning welcome in the south. Then they followed him to his stable yard which lay in the shadow of a great covered riding school.

One by one the candidates for sale were led into the yard, inspected and put through their paces, trotted back and forth. Horse of Destiny felt unfamiliar hands on him, a new face close to his own. The veterinary officer was measuring him and testing him for eye, wind and limb. Nothing wrong there. Army horses, say the specifications, must have a good action and be free of 'unsightly blemishes'. Household Cavalry horses have to be weight carriers, too. Horse of Destiny had more than all that. He had about him a pronounced look of breeding, he had presence, he had a touch of class. Colonel Spurrey nodded, a price was agreed, and, that first day of June, Horse of Destiny became the property of the British Army.

Mr Connors in the yard where the Army Purchasing Commission decided to buy Horse of Destiny. (The Author)

The veterinary officer took out his marking scissors and clipped the shape of a roman numeral in the shaggy hair on the side of his body, his first identification mark. It would soon grow out.

Five days later Horse of Destiny and the three dozen who had been bought with him were trundled into wagons and driven to the Dublin port of Dun Laoghaire, where they were staged in cattle lairages to await the ferry. No horse likes a new experience, because every new experience is filled with the alarm that goes with uncertainty, with the unknown. Had Horse of Destiny objected he would have been the first to make a fuss, to have kicked the pen and pulled incessantly at his headrope. But that June day the cattle-pen crossing over the choppy Irish sea was not too bad: not rough enough for him to complain.

At Holyhead they were disembarked into lairages to await the train – yet another strange experience – and next day they arrived in Leicestershire. Soon they reached the Army Veterinary Corps Centre at Melton Mowbray, home of the Army Schools of Equitation and Farriery and the Army Dog Training Centre, a place where the occasional howling of alsatians and labradors mingled with the clatter of horses. That evening found Horse of Destiny in a cosy loose-box, deep with straw, similar to the accommodation given him by Mr Connors during the fortnight preceding his sale to the Army, a regular luxury home after those bleak and dirty cattle pens.

The following morning he felt a needle in his neck, a tetanus and equine flu injection, and on his lower eyelid the prick of the mallein test, the safeguard against glanders. He was given a Bott powder and a worming powder, and he was led down to the forge – the finest forge in Britain – to have his Army number branded on his forefeet. As Horse of Destiny was the 5,816th remount to enter the Army in the current cycle, 5816 was the number allotted to him, the figure 5 being imprinted on his off-fore and 816 on his near fore. For the time being, therefore, we shall call him '5816'.

For the next five months 5816 would be under the supervision of Major Laycock, the Depot's Estate Stable Manager. In order to give any disease or disorder that may have been lurking in him a chance to become apparent, but not be passed on to his fellows, Major Laycock shut him up, for the next three weeks, in an isolation field. Thereafter, until November, 5816 idled away the hours on a larger paddock with some of his mates, a well-drained pasture with sturdy shelter against wet and windy nights.

The taste of Leicestershire grass was a novelty on his palate, not appreciably inferior to that of County Waterford, but essentially different, because, from the time he was weaned, Irish grass had been his only pasture diet, and Irish grass is unique. But there is a belt of country over that part of the Shires, stretching from Market Harborough to Oakham, through Melton Mowbray, which is said to contain the most productive fattening land in all England. Melton horses have always done extra well.

Every now and then he was brought in for further worming treatment, to be de-loused and to have his feet trimmed at the forge. He was not much disturbed; he had rich grazing and purest water a-plenty, all his needs were catered for.

Later that summer a representative from the Household Cavalry came up to Melton to cast an eye over the available and eligible horses. That day all those which the Purchasing Commission had bought from Ireland with the Household Cavalry in mind were earmarked to proceed to London in November to become 'Horses of the Queen'.

Down went 5816 to the Melton forge again, this time to have a pair of shoes nailed to his forefeet. These appendages, heavy, rigid and alien, felt strange for him, like a first pair of sandals might feel for a child. But in a day or two they were as second nature. When the month of November arrived, 5816 found himself being led up the ramp of a box again. He needed no lessons in that game now. People were already beginning to think of him as a creature that could do anything he chose, but one of whims, one that might always need winning round first. If some horses are gifted with a sense of adventure, perhaps 5816 had rather more than his share. If so, he must have felt that the journey upon which he now embarked was of rather special importance.

2 In the Hands of Trooper McGregor

So, for Household Cavalry remount 5816 the five months' interim at Melton Mowbray ended in November, 1967, when, with a pair of shoes on his front feet but none behind, and in the company of 25 other black geldings and mares and two greys – six horses to a box – he travelled to Wellington Barracks, London, to commence his six months' basic education.

Wellington Barracks, flanking Birdcage Walk, is right next to Buckingham Palace, the London home of Her Majesty the Colonel-in-Chief of the Household Cavalry, and immediately opposite St James's Park. By tradition it is a Foot Guards station but, between 1965 and 1970, while the old Victorian Hyde Park Barracks was being demolished and cleared away to make way for the new barracks, which were to be built to the design of Sir Basil Spence, Wellington was the home of the Household Cavalry Mounted Regiment.

A prefabricated riding school was erected in front of the Guards Chapel, while, at either end of Wellington's broad cream Regency front – a façade so familiar to Londoners walking in St James's Park or along Birdcage Walk – utility stables were built, those of The Life Guards Squadron being over to the left and those of the Royal Horse Guards (the Blues) on the right.

Wellington Barracks presented a sharp contrast to Melton Mowbray for 5816 and his companions. It was a place surrounded by the roar of traffic, resounding to the measured tread of marching soldiery and the strike of well-shod equine feet on tarmac, to the urgency of trumpet calls and words of command; it was a place where 200 horses were subjected to a close round-the-clock routine of reveille call, mucking out and grooming, watering and feeding, road exercise and troop drills, guard duty and riding school, rugging up and 'lights out'.

Number 5816 and his mates were unboxed that November morning in front of the Blues' stables, where the next stage of their lives was to be determined. Although in terms of bone 5816 was fully grown, notwithstanding the stark punctuation marks of his broad blaze and four white socks, you would scarcely have recognised a shadow of him in the old warrior you know today as, four years old, he clattered down the ramp of his horse-box that winter's morning. He not only had the wild and woolly appearance of an unclipped and dirty horse, but he was generally raw-looking, gangly, inflexible, head-in-the-air, clumsily coltish in his gait. And yet he stood out among his mates as a horse of quality.

The wild ancestors of 5816, were, by nature – like the troopers who were destined to ride them – gregarious beings. Thus a cavalry horse has a strong psychological advantage over many other members of his race, in that he enjoys the constant security of living and working cheek-by-jowl with his kith and kin. Company, to a horse, represents security. But, in contrast to cavalry troopers, the wild ancestors of 5816 led a lazy life, grazing, drinking sublimely at pool and riverside, roaming in search of fresh forage, mating, cavorting for the joy of living, and really only exerting themselves when they galloped away from danger.

For the likes of 5816, however, for the horse that is to be man's military servant, the energetic acts of roaming and cavorting and escaping are channelled into a life of closely disciplined work, a life that depends, not upon any breaking of spirit but upon total obedience. He had left behind the idle, carefree days, the days of browsing and gallivanting in verdant pastures.

The aims were to have him moving with continuous impulsion and even rhythm, and demonstrating, in all his activity, the correct bends. To create in him the ideal head carriage and neck curvature, flexy, nose down, bent at the poll; to train him to move at once with lightness and energy and to be instantly responsive to his rider's aids – in other words to the leg and hand signals by which the rider conveys his intentions. To have him totally steady on parade, imperturbable in his drill movements, and standing square and still when so requested. To make him, in short, a worthy representative of the smartest, the most elite mounted corps in the world.

The remount riders observed 5816 and his stable-mates with the critical eyes of schoolmasters surveying a new entry of students. Each of those trainers, hand-picked from their squadrons for the job, had completed, under the Royal Army Veterinary Corps at Melton Mowbray, a six months' course, during which time, in addition to studying and applying the principles of horsemastership, they had fully trained a half-trained horse and broken and schooled a raw remount. By the time 5816 reached Wellington, some of those who stood watching him had broken and schooled half-a-dozen and more horses since their training ended. They were men at once strong-minded and patient, hard and benign, inflexibly firm, yet kind and sensitive. They were the elite of the elite Household Cavalry.

When a new batch of horses arrived at Wellington, the 'rough riders' took their pick – just as they do annually at Windsor today – according to their seniority and length of service. A rider who chooses a horse with the looks of some blood and breeding may have a more difficult time breaking him than his colleague who selects the more common-looking animal. On the other hand he is likely to have the satisfaction of producing a more accomplished end-product. Any experienced eye could see that, below the ungainly outward appearance of 5816, stood a quadruped of potentially useful conformation.

But the eye – the eye of 5816 – that met those of the remount riders' showed a lot of white and not a little defiance. Such white and such expression in a horse's eye does not inspire complete confidence in the man whose lot it may be to break him. 5816 did not have a 'kind eye'. That is not to say that his eye was necessarily malevolent, or even wickedly mischievous. Perhaps, in his case, 'impish' would be the apt description. Impish, indeed, was his nature.

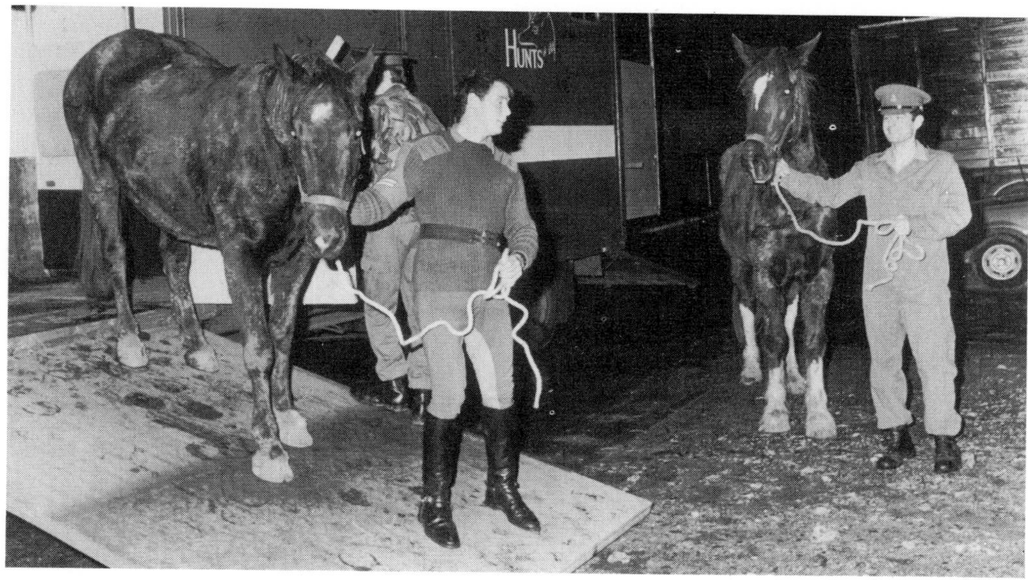

Household Cavalry remounts being unboxed following their journey from the Royal Army Veterinary Corps Depot at Melton Mowbray. (Mark Shearman)

Each remount rider would pick two horses, there being more than twice as many horses as trainers. So that, when every horsemaster had had one choice, there were enough horses for a second round. Trooper Douglas McGregor*, being fresh from the Melton Course, was the junior member of the Equitation Wing, and therefore had the last pick.

While the other remounts stood comparatively quiet, 5816, full of life and vigour as usual, was playing, sidestepping, dancing, rearing up a little on his hind legs. Despite his obvious air of quality he was not the choice of the first eleven riders. They selected quieter animals. That was just what McGregor had been hoping for. 'I was thanking my lucky stars he was still left. He looked to me as though he had more character than any of them . . . He was a bit of a show-off.'

So 5816 was McGregor's first selection. He was to reflect on that decision with very mixed feelings.

On the first morning McGregor took 5816 from his stall and, in the company of some of his stable-mates and their trainers, simply led him round the riding school, teaching him to walk up to his shoulder, the first exercise in rapport and obedience. After three or four days practising that initial discipline, he led him into the same arena wearing a cavesson. To this he attached a 25-foot canvas rein; and, with that rein at full length, he lunged 5816, invited him to describe circles around him, clockwise and anti-clockwise. His long whip never touched 5816, but occasionally it snaked out behind him with a whisper and a snap, urging the horse to advance or to increase his pace.

5816 had spent the summer grazing and the autumn mostly on hay. Now that work had begun in earnest his hay was supplemented with a couple of

* Now Squadron Corporal-Major McGregor, Warrant Officer of the Household Cavalry Equitation Wing.

(Left and opposite): *Corporal-Major (SQMC) Douglas McGregor, the Warrant Officer of the Household Cavalry's Equitation Wing, lungeing a remount at Combermere Barracks, Windsor, in 1983. In 1967, as Trooper McGregor, he had recently qualified as a remount rider, 5816 being the first Household Cavalry horse that he broke and made. (The Author)*

pounds of oats a day and half a pound of bran. This was a very dry diet, but he liked the novelty.

At this stage McGregor only walked him on the lunge, circling for a few minutes this way and a few minutes that, and only for half an hour a day. Since concentration is an acquired art, at first only a little of it was demanded of him. After a week he was persuaded to walk and trot and walk and stop, and walk and trot again, to the right and to the left, for an unremitting hour a day.

The objects of these preliminary exercises were to get him bending, to develop, strengthen, tension and flex his spine, to supple and muscle him all over and to persuade him to respond to the dictates of the human hand and voice. When he did what was wanted of him, several times in succession, he was rewarded with a handful of oats from his trainer's pocket. Docility is an important trait in the character of the horse. Provided he understands what is required of him and is educated correctly he will probably do all, within his capability, that is asked of him.

But 5816, with his touch of superior breeding, did not respond so willingly as most. While others submitted, more or less entirely, to this 'unnatural' treatment, he would often prance, suddenly spring forward, peevishly swish his tail or put in a little buck or two, to show his human mentor that he was not going to accept total domination.

Would he qualify as a ceremonial horse? It was by no means certain. What hung in the balance for 5816, just before Christmas, was the question of to which squadron he would be posted. Would it be to The Life Guards or the Royal Horse Guards? The problem was resolved in the usual way by the two Squadron Leaders. They tossed a coin for first pick, then they chose alternately down to the last of the 25 remounts. Major H. O. Hugh-Smith,* of the Royal Horse Guards, won against Major R. I. Ferguson†, of The Life Guards. Major Hugh-Smith selected number 5816 first go. That said much for McGregor's initial handling as well as for the horse's good looks.

* Afterwards lost a forearm in Northern Ireland; was Equerry to HRH The Duke of Edinburgh; and later commanded the Blues and Royals.
† All-England polo player and Executive of the Guards Polo Club.

It seemed to be the destiny of 5816, not only to be in the Blues, but to be in the forefront, too. Soon his off-fore would bear his regimental number, RHG 61, and, in a moment, he would be named. That year all the new horses received names beginning with the letter 'S'.

The name of 5816, as the Squadron Leader's first choice, was determined with care. He was called after Major the Earl of Sefton, an officer who joined the Royal Horse Guards in 1917 and spent the last year of the Great War in the front line. Lord Sefton was appointed Adjutant of the Blues in 1922. Although he retired in 1930, he rejoined in 1939, to serve with distinction in the Middle East until 1943.*

How difficult it would have been to imagine that the name 'Sefton', as given to a mere cavalry troop horse, might one day be echoed through the world.

Sefton was soon learning the environment and routine of a troop horse, everything being done by parades, like clockwork and by the clock. He was mucked out at reveille stables. His feed bin was tipped into his manger at the

* Among several other appointments, Lord Sefton held those of ADC to the Governor-General of Canada and to the Viceroy of India; he was a Lord-in-Waiting to King Edward VIII, and, afterwards, Lord Mayor of Liverpool.

same moment as his neighbours'. He was led out to the water troughs with the others, five or six at a time. Never having been clipped, he could not yet be groomed properly but only brushed superficially.

Each day he was taken out to continue his education in that makeshift indoor riding school next to the Guards Chapel. After McGregor had put him through his paces on the lungeing rein for another couple of weeks, he began the step-by-step process of accustoming him to a saddle and bridle.

First a breaking pad was secured to his back by a leather girth, then a blanket was introduced below the pad and a mouthing bit was placed in his mouth. Initially, he found the girth irritating and rather disconcerting but, gradually, he became accustomed to it. The bit was uncomfortable, especially when it knocked the bars of his mouth, those tender parts behind the bottom teeth, or when he got his tongue over the top of it. But in time he became used to the snaffle.

After he was walked and trotted around the school on the single lungeing rein, McGregor tried him on the side-reins which he attached first to a cavesson, then to a snaffle. At this stage the side-reins took the place of the rider's hands, while the whip curving out occasionally from behind the trainer's back, acted as a substitute for the rider's legs, urging Sefton all the time into contact with his bit. *Impulsion* was the key word in his schooling.

After a few weeks he sensed McGregor's body across his back, stomach downwards. He did not take kindly to that treatment. Next, for the first time, came the weight of a saddle behind his withers, and a running martingale to link his girth with his snaffle reins.

McGregor grew closer and closer to his horse. He gained his confidence by speaking to him soothingly and often, and rewarding him with tit-bits. Sefton returned McGregor's affection, and although he was by no means bowed, there was already a bond between them as close as human friends.

Now that Sefton was accustomed to a saddle he would not mind a rug on his back at night. That meant he could be clipped, and so, before the winter was through, his pristine hair was shaved. He made quite a fuss about that, especially when the clippers buzzed around his ears and the ticklish part of his girth and belly. The loss of that nice woolly coat caused him to shiver for a while, but the rug – the first garment he had ever worn, apart from boots and bandages – made him warm again. His mane was thinned, too, the first stage in helping it to lie smartly against his neck; tufts were pulled from his tail to give it shape, his feet were trimmed again, and he was taken down to the forge to have a pair of shoes fitted to his hind feet.

Already he had been asked to jump low obstacles, fitted against the long walls of the school: first the *cavaletti* poles set a few inches from the ground, then brush fences, three feet high. McGregor had guessed that Sefton, with his well-muscled, sloping shoulder and long reach, would make a fine jumper. So that was beginning to prove. He sprang over those obstacles with almost effortless ease.

It was March 1968. Sefton felt McGregor's weight astride the saddle on his back and sensed the stirrup-irons hanging at his side, while an assistant

The officer after whom 5816 was named: Captain (later Major) the Earl of Sefton as Adjutant of the Royal Horse Guards (the Blues) in the 1920s.

instructor had him on the lunge again, round and round, back and forth, clockwise and anti-clockwise, in those seemingly interminable bending, strengthening, suppling circles. Although, for the first time, he felt the strain of a burden, his back accepted it easily. After a while he was taken off the lunge and absolutely controlled by his trainer. Then he felt the urgent pressure of McGregor's legs, as the trainer held him on the bit, prompting him from behind the girth, 'collecting' him, persuading him to extend his trot, while he rose in the saddle in time with Sefton's fluent rhythm.

Before the end of the month Sefton was cantering, now on the near fore, now on the off fore. He was not asked to canter from a trot that became faster and faster, as a wild, or untrained horse, would begin to canter, but always from a controlled and disciplined trot. When McGregor drew back his right leg and squeezed strongly with both legs, the young gelding found himself going naturally into a left canter, and when McGregor drew back his left leg to the same accompaniment, Sefton struck off with the right. As for 'leaping', by now McGregor had him going down a lane of jumps as well as any 'Foxhunter' or 'Stroller'.

For some days now his trainer – dressed in the smart blue patrols, scarlet striped breeches, white cross-belt and red-banded forage cap of the London-based Household Cavalry remount rider – had been taking him out on the traffic-hectic streets early in the morning in the company of another horse and trainer. Sefton had been getting used, from afar, to that constant rush surrounding Wellington Barracks. Now he experienced it too close for comfort, and, owing to his sensitive, high-mettled nature he found it less easy to live with than did his fellows. These loud, shiny metal creatures accelerated, one after another, as they overtook him and his trainer. They changed gear just behind him, their exhausts exploded, their horns sounded, their brakes screeched, their engines revved up at the traffic lights, while their remorseless flow, this way and that, was all too nerve-racking for young Sefton. He was easily upset by sudden, unexpected movements. But for the powerful flow of confidence and reassurance coming through to him by way of McGregor's leg and arm and soothing voice, he would have lost his self-control. With a less capable rider he would almost certainly have bolted in terror. '*Who-a now! There, boy, there!*'

About this time, too, he was tried on the lateral movements, and he took them in his stride. Soon he could demonstrate the shoulder-in and the half pass, he turned nicely on the forehand and pirouetted in smooth style (when he felt so inclined). Now, by way of variety, McGregor was teaching him to step over poles spaced evenly on the ground. This exercise was designed to supple him further, to induce an even length of stride and teach him to pick up his feet, stepping smartly.

His next test was the State bit, another legacy from the days of the old war-horse, from the time when the horse soldier needed close, and immediate control of his steed's head, so that his right arm was free to wield the sword or lance. The Household Cavalry horse wears the State bit in combination with the decorative breastplate, bright-chain and sheepskin-covered saddle, on all ceremonial occasions from the Queen's Life Guard to the Queen's Birthday Parade. The bit is in two parts, a bridoon, which is controlled by an upper rein, and a curb on the lower rein. The jointed bridoon, working on the corners of Sefton's mouth, had a similar action to the snaffle which he carried almost as second nature now. But the curb is a potentially severe instrument. Its heavy, straight, white-metal mouthpiece rested either side of his lower jaw, behind his teeth, on the bars of his mouth, the sensitive portion of his lower mouth that was devoid of teeth. The long, S-shaped cheeks of the bit rotated when McGregor shortened the rein, and Sefton did not like that. He also felt, behind his lower lip, a flat chain, the curb-chain, which was attached, near either end of the bar of the curb, to the upper cheek of the bit.

When the State headkit is worn, the bridoon rein is slack, the horse being ridden on the curb. Household Cavalrymen are taught to use the State bit with due care, without causing pain or unnecessary discomfort. Nevertheless, it lay disconcertingly heavy in Sefton's mouth now, and he reared to show his objection.

A horse is very sensitive to pain. Unlike a dog he has little facial expression to convey his feelings. Nor can he howl like a dog. He is an animal of flight. The instinct of a horse who suffers is to flee, thinking he can thereby escape the torment. A horse who has been broken to saddle and bridle, and who suffers, may endeavour to detach himself from his accoutrements and 'escape'. He may try to unseat his rider, and while the rider's hand prevents him from actually bolting, he will try the next best thing, 'double quick mark time' at the trot or canter, or he will rear.

Was it mainly the ironmongery in Sefton's mouth that made him so restless, or was there something else wrong? Hock and foot trouble often come to light from the pressure of work on a green young horse. Perhaps some injury or strain in that quarter was upsetting him? The Veterinary Officer took a look at Sefton's legs and hooves. Yes, there were slight signs of unsoundness. He was duly treated and rested. But it made little difference to his demeanour. Was it simply that he was determined to remind his mentor, from time to time, that, underneath that sleek black coat, he still possessed a fiery independent spirit, one that was never to be totally subdued?

He was now regarded as the maverick of his intake. Yet McGregor found him a most stimulating companion.

In those days there was a Household Cavalry remount competition, staged at the Windsor Horse Show. In 1968 it was judged by a former Blues officer, the Duke of Beaufort, Master of the Horse to the Queen, and a former Life Guards officer, Lieutenant-Colonel Sir Rupert Hardy. It was a simple test for Sefton, because the remounts were only led in hand and judged on looks and action. It was a triumphant day for him, too. He was placed second to a Life Guards horse. His squadron leader, Major Hugh-Smith, swears to this day that he should have been first!

Now it was time for the remounts' final trial – the Remount Pass Out. At the end of May they were ridden into the riding school, half-a-dozen at a time, to 'face the music'. For, unless a Household Cavalry horse can stand a brass band and cheering crowds, he will have no future in the ceremonial role. As Sefton and his companions went through the big double doors, half-a-dozen at a time, they were confronted, in the middle of the tan floor, by a group of bandsmen, playing with full gusto and accompanied by some rowdy troopers, shaking brooms and waving handkerchiefs. Clearly Sefton thought this cacophony was nothing less than a gross insult to the equine race. McGregor had a terrible tussle with him, all the time prancing and attempting to canter, to bolt, to get as far away from the dreadful racket as he could, or suddenly stopping in his tracks, turning his head furiously at the musicians and snorting his disapproval.

All the remounts, except poor Sefton, were passed out, qualified as troop horses. He was in disgrace. McGregor was bitterly disappointed.

Band practice in the riding school. On either side are remount horses being accustomed to the noise. (Mike Roberts)

3 How to Disgrace the Queen's Birthday Parade

Notwithstanding his failure at the Remount Pass Out, early in June Sefton took part in the world's greatest and most resplendent annual military parade: Trooping the Colour.

The Queen's Birthday Parade has always been looked upon as the remounts' ultimate post-graduate trial, the apex of their training, and, although Sefton had failed the Pass Out, it was hoped that the Trooping's long trial of fortitude and patience, with its two rehearsals, amounting to three three-hour ordeals on three successive Saturdays, would help accustom him to ceremonial noise and public clamour and the discomfort of the State bridle. That apart, the Household Cavalry is always stretched almost to the limit to find sufficient horses for the Birthday Parade; every available sound horse is called upon to fill the commitment. Sefton was needed.

Trooping the Colour is, fundamentally and originally, a Foot Guards occasion whose tradition stems from the 17th century, when all Britain's major garrison towns became the scene of a ceremonial guard mounting parade, with due honour being paid to the regimental and company Colours. In London, from the mid-18th century, guards were mounted over the Monarch and other members of the Royal Family and, when a guard went on parade, the Colour – having been blessed and dedicated by a priest and presented by the Sovereign, or his delegate – was duly 'trooped' down the ranks. Horse Guards Parade has been the scene of such dazzling ritual since the time of Charles II, when Sefton's black antecedents first clattered across the parade-ground's cobblestone paths.

In London the occasion was rendered, by degrees, a more impressive public spectacle by increasing its strength from all the Foot Guards' battalions stationed there; and now, in the summer months, the battalions of the Household Division frequently mount their guards from that huge space of ground. The parade that celebrates the Queen's Birthday is an extension of the same ritual.

Traditionally, the Household Cavalry have always provided their Monarch with a Sovereign's Escort for the Trooping, a force divided into four divisions, two from each of the Mounted Squadrons. Including the mounted band and the Queen's Life Guard (who turn out, mounted, in Horse Guards forecourt to salute the Queen Mother as she alights there from her carriage) a total of 191 horses are needed. In 1968, the year of Sefton's Trooping, it was a Life Guards escort, that is to say it was under command of the Major

Horse Guards Parade has been the scene of such dazzling ritual since the time of Charles II.'

commanding The Life Guards squadron and The Life Guards Standard was carried.

The Trooping was to be the embodiment of everything that Sefton seemed to dislike most: brass bands, much sudden rush and noise, the sway of a sword scabbard against his side and, above all, the heavy discomfort of the State bit. How would he get on? No one was more concerned with that question than Trooper McGregor.

For the two rehearsals, the first taken by the Major-General Commanding the Household Division and the second by the Foot Guards' senior regimental Colonel, the Duke of Gloucester, he was manageable. But how would he be on the big day when the sides of the Mall would be thronged with cheering crowds, and the atmosphere around Horse Guards Parade charged with emotion?

For him the day began at 5.30 am when McGregor took him into the riding school and, in the company of half-a-dozen others, put him through thirty minutes' trot to settle him down. Then he was returned to his stall, watered and fed – Sefton was now on a daily ration of four-and-a-half pounds of oats, two-and-a-half pounds of cereal nuts, half-a-pound of bran and four haynets – after which McGregor, not without misgivings, went off for his own breakfast.

At 8.30, all up and down the troop stalls where Sefton lived, there began a bustle of grooming: first the dandy brush, which massages the hide and loosens the dirt, then the body brush and curry comb, in relentless arm-sweeping rhythm; then the sponging of the eyes, nostrils and dock, the combing of the mane and brushing out of the tail, the picking and oiling of the feet, the chalking of the four white socks and afterwards the final wisp and rubber, the ultimate gloss. Never before had Sefton received such close and dedicated attention; never before, in the eyes of men, had he appeared so handsome. By the time his saddle, with its black sheepskin piled high over

A drum horse of the Blues, from the painting by Charles Stadden.

the front arch, and his State bridle were on, with his prominent T-shaped white blaze and socks, he looked a picture.

The escort formed up on the expansive barrack square before the façade of Wellington Barracks, the mounted band in their gold-lace State coats and velvet caps on the left, The Life Guards with their scarlet jackets and white plumes in the middle, and the Blues caparisoned in dark blue with crimson plumes on the right, a spectacle of dazzling colour, of glittering cuirasses and helmets, deep-shine jackboots and glowing black horses. McGregor's eyes, looking between Sefton's ears, peered from behind the sharp 'V' peak of his helmet whose point lay almost against his nose. When Sefton tossed his head, champing at the heavy bit, the silver bright-chain that encircled his neck shook and jingled, and when he swished his tail and stamped his feet, McGregor gave him the leg squeeze that told him to be still.

The period of enforced immobility appeared to be without end; the inspection seemed to take so much longer than it had before the two rehearsals. But at last the Adjutant came to the division in which Sefton stood, the third division, completing his scrutiny with the backsides of the fourth division. And so, with drawn swords, the Escort walked out in column of sections for Buckingham Palace, in front of which its four divisions formed up on the road, The Life Guards in front, the Blues behind.

At 10.45 Her Majesty, Colonel-in-Chief of all the Guards regiments, horse and foot, romantically elegant in scarlet tunic, dark-blue side-saddle and plumed tricorne hat, and followed by her Consort, HRH Prince Philip, Duke of Edinburgh, turned out as Colonel of the Welsh Guards, together with her entourage, passed the ranks of her Household Cavalry. The crowds at the Palace railings waved their flags and shouted till they were hoarse, while Sefton, to make his opinion of the ugly hubbub plainly known, stamped up and down and raised himself on his hind legs. As the divisions of the Escort began to take their place in the procession's tail, however, McGregor managed to wheel him into column. But going down the rose-red Mall, with a wide space between each horse and rider, the sea of noisy civilian faces behind the policemen and the stamping and presenting arms by the Foot Guards' street-liners, coupled with the tall fluttering row of banners that flanked the road, soon became intolerable to the young horse.

He kept breaking into a trot, and even into a canter, when he should have been at a sedate walk; and, every now and again, when there was a sudden movement, he would shy and dance in the ranks. He was already proving a grave embarrassment to the Household Cavalry.

As the glittering escort's *clip-clop* ended, when its four divisions swung into line before the Guards Memorial, the clock over Horse Guards arch, now facing them, beat its 11 o'clock chimes. Directly below it, Her Majesty turned to her right, and the massed bands of the Brigade of Guards suddenly struck into *God Save the Queen*; and what with the shouting of the Foot Guards officer commanding the parade, the sea of scarlet tunics and black bearskins, the clatter of the rifles and the drum of the heels of several hundred men on the gravel, Sefton's alarm was acute. Everything seemed to be flash and explosion today, the worst assault on his ears and eyes and nerves he had ever known – infinitely worse than being ridden around the motor-hectic streets of Victoria and Pimlico.

The Queen rode out to inspect her Guards, traversing the length of the front rank, then circling behind their lines to cast an appraising eye over her Household Cavalry, while all the time, to Sefton's agitation and McGregor's consternation, the massed bands of the Brigade of Guards, drawn up in front of Downing Street, played their stirring, riotous marches.

The Queen must have seen the young horse, with the big white blaze and the four white socks, break the stillness of the third division's line with his prancing and his attempts to back out of his rank; and so, as they rode behind her, would her Gold Stick-in-Waiting for that day, Admiral of the Fleet Earl Mountbatten of Burma, Colonel of The Life Guards, Field-Marshal Sir Gerald Templer, the Colonel of the Blues, and her Master of the Horse, the Duke of Beaufort (who had so recently helped to place Sefton second in the remounts class at Windsor). Of course Sefton was not the only horse that would not stand rock still as his Queen rode by, but his conduct was easily the worst.

Following Her Majesty's inspection the stillness was broken by the shrieking of human voices, the blare of brass instruments and the chorus of tramping feet against a multi-coloured sea of thousands of civilians sitting shoulder to shoulder in the high-raised stands, in front of Horse Guards and facing inwards before Downing Street and the Admiralty. There was the march and counter-march of the Foot Guards' massed bands; then, preceded by a series of drum-taps, the collection of the Colour by the Ensign; and to more raucous music, the march past of the eight guards, first in slow time, then in quick time, nearly an hour-long bedlam, a frenetic rigmarole sufficient to test the imperturbability of any green horse, let alone one of the sensitivity of Sefton.

He hated every moment of it. He had got himself so worked up that lines of lather showed up as frothy white as shaving soap under his breastplate and, as he tossed his head, in annoyance at his heavy bit, the foam flecked back from his champing mouth like the foam of the waves of a stormy sea, onto McGregor's cuirasses and onto that pointed peak of McGregor's helmet. *Steady boy. Steady*! the remount rider muttered again and again. He had ridden Sefton for seven months. No one in the world could have held him better that day.

To his relief it was now the turn of the Sovereign's Escort to play its part in the proceedings: first the march past on Horse Guards parade, then the rank past, the taking leave of Her Majesty at Buckingham Palace. The marathon would soon be over. *Household Cavalry, car-ry swords! To the right, form column of troops, walk march*! The Life Guards band struck up, their skewbald drum horse in the lead, and away went the four divisions towards Downing Street with all the brave grandeur of an 18th century squadron of horse riding into battle. They turned left at the corners of the great parade-ground, twice past the Queen, initially at the walk then at the trot, to the accompaniment of the cavalry music that would one day be so familiar to Sefton's ears: *Aida* and *The Keel Row, Bonnie Dundee* and *Monymusk*. And while the Escort advanced in straight and serried ranks, nearly every head and tail lined up as one, experienced eyes everywhere were noticing that, in the third Division, there was a horse that *would not behave*. They did not know that he was called Sefton, that his name would one day resound through the world.

For all his boisterousness, shyness of noise and resistance to the curb, Sefton was a horse of such character, such presence and style, that everyone was determined that he should eventually make the grade. After all, that rearing habit only occurred when he held the big bar of the State bit in his mouth, and while the scabbard bounced against his near side. Surely it was only a matter of time before he accepted those appendages as second nature? McGregor worked on him every day, and, after another three months, the recalcitrant gelding seemed to grow used to the bit, the scabbard became a habit, the London noises meant less and less to him. On September 15, McGregor rode into the riding school to face the Remount Pass Out again. This time Sefton passed it – just. At last he was a fully-fledged Royal Horse Guards troop horse, and McGregor, with mixed feelings, proud and happy, but poignant, too, bade him good-bye.

(Above) The Queen's Birthday Parade: The Household Cavalry march past.

Photo: Mike Roberts

2. *(Below)* The stables at Horse Guards: 'This scene, with its antiquity and the echoes of its high vaulting, was altogether grander, more evocative of the old horsed cavalry.'

Photo: Mike Roberts

3. Whitehall: the changing of the Queen's Life Guard. 'The ritual is intricate, majestically dignified, richly emblematic of Britain's past.'
Photo: Leslie Lane

ARTISTS' IMPRESSIONS OF SEFTON

4 Captain Haworth-Booth's presentation picture (by Christine Bousfield) on his retirement from the Mastership of the Weser Vale Bloodhounds in 1973.

5. Saddled for Queen's Life Guard, 1983, by Elizabeth Lloyd. This picture was commissioned by the Author, and sold by him in aid of the Charitable Fund of the Household Cavalry Mounted Regiment.

SEFTON

Elizabeth Lloyd 1983

6. Sefton on sentry duty.
Photo: Mike Roberts

7. The Household Cavalry camped at Stoney Castle, Surrey 1982, by John King.

8. A competitor riding one of Sefton's stable mates in a tent pegging event. Sefton enjoyed a long career as a tent pegging horse.
Photo: Mike Roberts

9. Household Cavalry Bandsmen playing for the opening ceremony of a musical ride.
Photo: Mike Roberts

10. 'Rough-Riding instructors in Hyde Park, smart as whips in blue patrol tunics and scarlet-striped breeches.'
Photo: Mike Roberts

Members of the Queen's Life Guard during an adjutant's inspection. 'Finding the minutest imperfections . . . faults probably imperceptible to the lay eye.'
Photo: Mike Roberts

12. Crosses, flowers and horseshoes opposite the place of the explosion. 'Animal lovers would not forgive – not in a thousand years.'
Photo: Mike Roberts

13. *(Above)* Part of the Household Cavalry's musical ride, Horse of the Year Show, 1982. 'With the IRA iniquity very fresh in everyone's memories, the commentator reminded the audience of the valorous and noble character of the war horse.'

Photo: Mike Roberts

14. *(Below)* 'The spotlight was bear on the entrance, and in came Sefton, led by Pedersen '

Photo: Mike Ro

4 On Queen's Life Guard, then Failed Again

Sefton was now qualified to go on Queen's Life Guard, which, in the late 1960s, implied a relatively short journey: from Wellington Barracks, around the Victoria Memorial, the 'Wedding Cake', down the Mall, across Horse Guards Parade, under the arch, and onto the Horse Guards forecourt.

There, alternating just as they do now, The Life Guards and the Blues changed Guard every morning at 11 o'clock. When Her Majesty was in London the Guard to which Sefton would belong was composed of an officer – usually a Captain or Lieutenant – a corporal-major*, who carried the Royal standard, a trumpeter and 13 non-commissioned officers and troopers. When she was away from London it comprised a Corporal-of-Horse†, in command, and ten other ranks.

The Guard produced the two mounted sentries, occupying the tall and familiar stone boxes facing onto Whitehall, and two dismounted sentries. To be allotted a box was a great privilege, an honour given to the best four turn-outs, rider and horse, in the Guard. Box or no box, Sefton would stand resplendently in the public eye; for the Household Cavalry's Guard changing is always a popular occasion. At that time of year his rider wore the big blue cavalry cloak, with the scarlet collar, that reached well behind the saddle to keep not only himself warm, but Sefton's loins too, on a frosty morning.

The ritual is intricate, solemn, majestically dignified, richly emblematic of England's military past. When the Queen is in London and the trumpeters are on parade, the trumpeter of the Old Guard, the Guard in occupation, rides out of the forecourt onto Horse Guards Parade, and when he sees the New Guard approaching, he sounds the *General Parade*. On the stroke of 11 o'clock the New Guard rides under the arch, giving an *eyes left*, and a *Royal Salute* from their trumpeter, as they pass the Standard of the Old Guard, who are lined up with their backs to the Guard Room.

The New Guard manoeuvres from column into line, facing the Old Guard; the trumpeters, both on grey horses, sound the Royal Salute in unison, while the two officers salute with their swords, and thus the handover of duties and premises, and the changing of sentries, begins.

Sefton, experiencing this pomp and circumstance for the first time that autumn of 1968, went through the motions easily, and when his rider (an experienced rider for a horse with a doubtful reputation) dismounted in the

* In other regiments his equivalent is a sergeant-major.

† In other regiments his equivalent is a sergeant.

Sefton and rider ready for Queen's Life Guard. 'At that time of year his rider wore the big blue cavalry cloak with the scarlet collar, which reached well down behind the saddle'. (The Standard)

high-walled stable yard, he breathed a long sigh of relief. Sefton had behaved fairly well.

The Horse Guards, Whitehall, was a strange new environment for Sefton, one that he would get to know quite well during the next few weeks. Black horses of the Household Cavalry, horses such as Sefton, had mounted guard at Whitehall for over three centuries. For a century and a half this was the

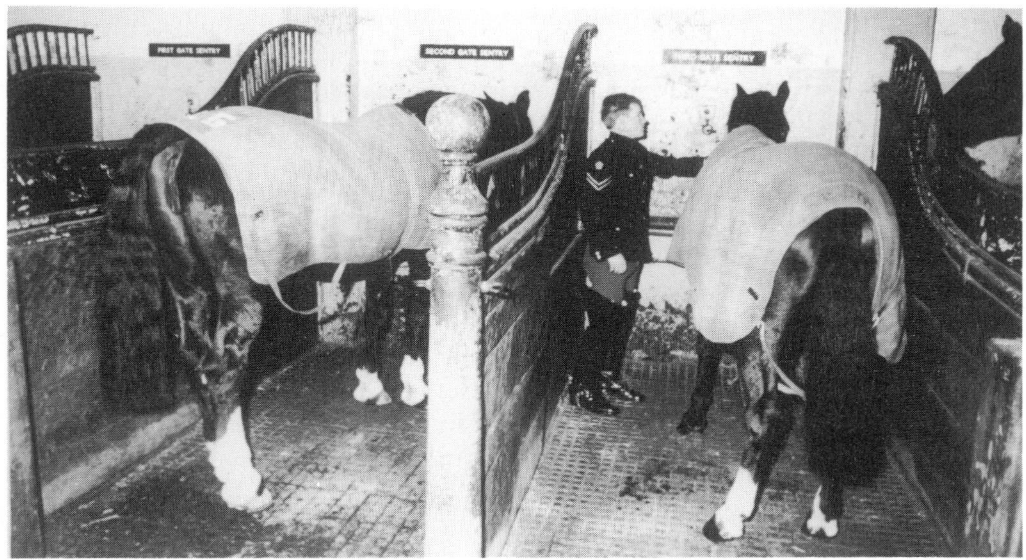

Horses of the Life Guards in their Whitehall stalls. (Mike Roberts)

preserve of The Life Guards, they being the only regiments* of Household Cavalry until the Royal Horse Guards (the Blues) were raised to that status in 1820. When The Life Guards were officially established as Charles II's bodyguard, in 1660, Whitehall Palace, which Henry VIII had wrested from Cardinal Wolsey in the previous century, was at once the Sovereign's residence and the seat both of Court and government.

The Palace bestrode the broad road called Whitehall, that now links Trafalgar Square to Parliament Square. The Life Guard sentries occupied boxes either side of the Palace's entrance, the Holbein Gate, which, if it had survived, would stand in the middle of that road, facing up towards Charing Cross, less than 50 yards from the present boxes. Thus it is at the Holbein Gate that the heritage of Sefton, as a Household Cavalry horse, began.

Whitehall Palace was burned down towards the end of the reign of William and Mary, a disaster obliging them to move to St James's. But the

* The 1st and 2nd Life Guards were amalgamated in 1922.

(Right and overleaf) *The stables at Whitehall. (Mike Roberts)*

Sovereign's Life Guard did not move. A new guard house was built for them on the present site. People often question why the Guard to which Sefton then belonged, the Guard symbolic of the protection of Her Majesty's person, is still at Whitehall. The answer is that the Horse Guards remains technically and traditionally the gateway to Royal London. Until well into the 19th century – Trafalgar Square and Admiralty Arch were not built until after 1840 – St James's Park with its Royal aviary, founded by Charles II, was generally inaccessible to the public. Still no vehicle can be taken through the Horse Guards gateway unless the driver or passenger is in possession of an Ivory Pass, a privilege granted to few. It is the principal duty of the Household Cavalry dismounted sentries to check Ivory Passes and to deny access to those not in possession of them.

During George III's reign it was ordained that there should be 'a new building for Her Majesty's Horse and Foot Guards' and, early in the 1750s, the clean, pale-grey lines of the Horse Guards we know today – the Headquarters of the Army's London District and the Household Division – were duly fashioned to the design of the leading architect, William Kent, with, at the east end, spacious quarters and stabling for The Life Guards, the first guardians of Royal London. The main offices of the Horse Guards were occupied by the Secretary of State for War and the Commander-in-Chief of the Army and their staffs, until 1856, when the Brigade of Guards took them over entirely.

The Horse Guards from Whitehall. Sefton occupies the sentry-box on the right. (Mike Roberts)

Just above that arch under which Sefton walked for the first time that autumn morning – his black coat wisped to shine like broken coals, his mouth working on the weight of the ceremonial bit – as William Kent's clock struck 11.0, were the offices of the commander of the whole of the Household Cavalry,* his adjutant and his clerks. The Commanding Officer of the Household Cavalry also holds the Court post of Silver Stick-in-Waiting, an

* The Corps' tank and armoured car regiments, though not within his operational command, are under his regimental administrative supervision.

appointment going back to the time of Titus Oates and the Popish Plot, when the Duke of Monmouth, Charles II's son, who was not only Captain-General of the King's army, but also in direct command of the Household Cavalry, recommended to his father to let him or one of The Life Guards captains

> attend on the King's person on foot, wheresoever he walks, from his rising to his going to bed, immediately next to the King's own person before all others, carrying in his hand an ebony staff or truncheon with a gold head, engraved with his Majesty's cipher and crown ... near him another principal commissioned officer, with an ebony staff and silver head, who is ready to relieve the Captain on all occasions.

In 1968 the two Gold Sticks, military figureheads and totems, high-powered reminders of the proximity of the Household Cavalry to the Queen, were Lord Mountbatten, Colonel of The Life Guards and Field Marshal Sir Gerald Templer, Colonel of the Royal Horse Guards (the Blues), both of whom, with her, had witnessed Sefton's monkeying on the Trooping.

Sefton, at five years old still highly impressionable, sniffed suspiciously around the whole unfamiliar atmosphere of the Horse Guards edifice: the tall, arched stables, the thick grey Portland stone, saturated with the vapours of horse urine and horse sweat and London pollution, the wall corners chipped and bruised by generations of kicks and knocks, the circles of erosion round the rusty wall-rings, the flagstones under the arch, sunk, like a Roman road, by many generations of black horses.

For a moment he had become part of that eternal scene: the pungent stable odours, the wall brackets that have always carried the sheepskin-covered saddles and the black-and-gold bridles, with their silver bright-chains in a figure of eight across their front; the hooks that have served generations for slings and sword-belts and scabbards; the piles of horse rugs, the mice scuttling between the feed bins, the water trough ('presented by the Drinking Fountain and Cattle Trough Association'), the loose-boxes with the labels for their three respective special horses – 'Captain of the Queen's Life Guard', 'Warrant Officer' and 'Trumpeter' – the vaulted echoing stalls with their iron-railing tops and their plaques for the Corporal-of-Horse, the junior NCO, the box sentries, the sentries 'over the arms' and the gate sentries.

Household Calvalry activity at Whitehall includes the dressing and smartening up for the officer's inspection at four o'clock (a parade instituted after the Guard had turned out drunk on an occasion when Queen Victoria drove through at that time in the afternoon). Every day it was the same: a full-dress inspection, with the minutest corrections made, here a helmet peak that did not come down to the nose, there a waist-belt buckle that bore a flick of tarnish, here a flask cord whose frayed end peeped out, there a sword-arm that was dropped from the parallel.

There was the bustle of morning and evening stables, the reverberation of hay forks and curry combs, the intermittent clip of the horses' feet and the urgent injunctions of the NCOs: '*Another haynet wanted here ... Time to mix the feeds ... This one's on bran mash ... Headcollar chain's come undone there ... Let's get Sefton's rug straightened up, shall we ...?*

At last, *Feed Away*! And, when the horses were bedded down, there was the quiet tramp of the stable guard, the occasional rattle of a headcollar chain or a horse's snort and the lights twinkling on the saddlery. This scene, with the echoes of the high vaulting and the very antiquity of the place, was altogether grander, more picturesque, more evocative of the old horsed cavalry, than it was in the barracks.

Alas, Sefton did not share that unique aura for much longer. Soon he was up to his old tricks, rearing and prancing and jiggering about. One day, when Corporal-of-Horse Stamford was riding him back to barracks with the Guard from Whitehall, he tried to break into a gallop; and, when the Guard formed up in Wellington Barracks, he reared so high that he toppled over backwards, Stamford sprawling across the parade-ground tarmac with an awful clatter of helmet and sword.

That, for the moment, was the end of Sefton as a ceremonial horse. He was in disgrace again. He was relegated to carrying recruits.

The Queen's Life Guard giving an 'eyes left' to the accompaniment of their Trumpeter's royal salute as they leave the Horse Guards after handing over their duties to the New Guard. The horse on the extreme left, throwing his head, is Sefton. (Leslie Lane)

5 Instructing the Recruits

By the first week of 1969 Sefton, himself so recently a 'recruit', was helping the Equitation Staff to teach soldier recruits how to ride. Some of those young men had been astride a horse in civilian life, and had enjoyed the experience sufficiently to apply for one of the Household Cavalry regiments. Others, a little older, who had volunteered for mounted duty from the service regiments – the tank and armoured car elements of the Household Cavalry – may have had some riding at Windsor or in Germany. But the recruit rides were mainly composed of youths, aged 18 to 20, who had never been in the saddle in their lives.

By comparison with many other army careers, the Household Cavalry offers wonderful prospects for civilian life. The Mounted Police, for example, welcome mature Household Cavalrymen who have served successful stints as mounted dutymen. Then again, with the horse becoming even more popular in Britain, there are all sorts of openings in the world of equestrianism. As most Household Cavalrymen were on short-term engagements, having signed on for six or nine years, as distinct from the more deeply committed 22, there was then, as there still is, a brisk turnover.

At the time Sefton became a riding-school horse, there were at Wellington Barracks four rides, each of 12 to 15 men, undergoing 20 weeks training. Their programme was intensive. Every weekday, besides the routine reveille stables, morning and evening stables and kit cleaning parade, those recruits spent an hour on the barrack square, with their swords, learning cavalry drill and, according to their equestrian progress, an hour, an hour-and-a-half or two hours in the riding school.

Within a few days of their posting to a troop they were shown how to muck out, how to mix feeds and fill haynets, how to lead a horse to water and how to groom him. By the end of the first week's training they had learned how to fit saddlery, how to saddle a horse and, beginning with the simple snaffle, how to bridle him. They were aware that quiet handling and a kind, yet confident, approach were the first requirements of sound horsemastership and successful equitation. Then they were taught how to mount and dismount; they were shown the correct position of hands, seat and legs, in simple terms how the 'aids' functioned, and when their stirrup leathers should be adjusted short and when long. Meanwhile they experienced the rigours of oft-repeated balance and agility exercises at the walk. They had begun to trot, too.

In the next step their instructor taught them how to turn and circle their horses at the walk. By the conclusion of their second week, they were cantering, and they were even beginning to wake to the reveille trumpet call

A senior ride getting the feel of some items of full dress. 'By now Sefton had learned that, in the world of horsemanship – yes, even the Household Cavalry was no exception – some riders feel a good deal more comfortable and au fait *on your back than others.' (Leslie Lane)*

without stiff and aching muscles. In the third and fourth weeks they were turning, circling, and vaulting onto their horses at the trot; in the fifth they received their first jumping lesson – over a single fence, 18 inches high, set against the school's long wall. In the sixth week they were jumping multiple fences, quite often with their arms folded; by the seventh, they were riding two hours a day; and in the eighth, they were out on the roads, learning road discipline. The following four weeks were spent practising troop drills in Hyde Park.

By then they knew that long, high-ceilinged riding school next to the Guards Chapel at Wellington Barracks as well as any of them wanted to know it, and some of them knew the positive, unrelenting, echoing voice of their rough-riding instructor so well that they were mimicking him in their sleep: *Quickest and best, mount! Adjust your reins! From the right, form single file, walk march! At the board, leading file to the left!... Watch the position of your head, that man on Sefton, head down, chin in!*

The recruits had so much to learn, such a variety of detail to absorb, so much new physical coordination to master – cavalry drill as well as all the fundamentals of horsemastership and equestrianism – that there was not much space in their minds and hearts for their horses as individual creatures. They had not yet found the capacity to give them the sort of affection and genuine respect that McGregor had given Sefton.

Nearly every day now Sefton was saddled up, led out and mounted by hands and legs he recognised as much clumsier than McGregor's; far less confident hands, less concerned with him, Sefton, as a flesh-and-blood being who could sense pain and pleasure, discomfort and luxury, sadness and joy, who was just as capable as any trooper of delighting in life or abhorring it.

He was always one to demand respect, and that was the year, 1969, when he began to earn a squadron reputation for making his feelings known. If his girth was buckled with too much of a jerk, or his bridle was not properly fitted; if his curb chain was too tight, his feet not properly picked out, or his bit jammed harshly into his mouth; if he was not led out of his stall with due care, or was made to hurry at the water trough, or if he was pushed around too roughly on grooming parades, he would wriggle and stamp, jerk his head up, put in a little buck, or, if really provoked, a jab with a hind foot. Recruits were learning that, while they could afford to be fairly cavalier with most of the 'blacks', Sefton was a law unto himself. He was an impatient horse, too. Anticipating the times when the bins of corn and bran and chaff were to be lined up behind each stall, on the dot, he was usually the first, jealously, to lay his ears back and to paw the ground.

Every working morning he was lined up with a dozen or more other riding school horses, while their recruits – wearing black butcher boots, khaki breeches and tunics, or later, full dress – faced in towards their horses' heads, holding them, elbows up, either side of the bridle, for the instructor's inspection. Branded as a rather difficult horse, Sefton was allotted to one of the senior rides, either to the top 'khaki ride', or to the 'kit' (full dress) ride, so that a relatively experienced recruit should have him. But experience is not everything. Some of those trainees, by the time they progressed to Sefton, had emerged as quite safe horsemen; others were less strong, less adept, less safe. A horse who had been accustomed to McGregor's supple strength, expert guiding hands and legs and unusual horse-sense, found the antics of those tyros disconcerting.

So, by now, Sefton had learned that, in the world of horsemanship – yes, even the Household Cavalry is no exception – some riders feel a good deal more comfortable and *au fait* on one's back than others. He and the instructors had effective ways and means of dealing with the hesitant, the feeble, the inept and the idle: *Ride, take up your reins! At the quarter marker, right incline! Ride, quit and cross your stirrups! From the front tell off by sections! Flanks of sections, prove!... Ride, ter-rot! Smith, you're flopping about like a sack of potatoes, you are, sit upright, lad! There, that's better...* The ride continues circling round the school, stamping down the tan, tight against the wall, while, occasionally, a man's foot, or a horse's foot rings against the boards, echoing to the vaults.

Number one section, at the half marker right turn! Turn and change!... Come on, Jones, you're too slow on the change... Ride, near fore leading, canter!... Who's that on Sefton? Clark!... Shorten your reins! How many times do I have to tell you? You must maintain contact with his mouth, man. Come on now, elbows in, heels down, sit right down in the saddle, or Sefton'll have you off... There look at you, on your arse on the tan, I told you you couldn't take liberties with that horse... Ride, trot! Ride, wa-a-alk! Go on, Clark, catch Sefton, take him into the middle of the school and get mounted... Now join your section, lad... Ride, make much of your horses!

Sword drill in the riding school. (Leslie Lane)

And, along with the others, the man whom Sefton has pitched onto the floor gives him a grateful pat on the neck.

In the thirteenth week the horses wore universal bits; service swords – that is, pre-War fighting swords – were fitted to their saddles, and mounted sword drill was the order of the day. By the fourteenth and fifteenth weeks the recruits were approaching *haute école*, learning collection and extension, receiving bending lessons, shoulder in and shoulder out, and half-pass to the right and left. In the sixteenth week they were shown up, put through their paces before their Commanding Officer and passed out, or not, as the case might be.

The seventeenth week found them in those white leather gauntlets and breeches, stiff, winged jackboots, helmets and cuirasses that are unique to their Corps, and then, once again, Sefton felt the State bit lying heavy in his mouth, the bit to which, coupled with the curb, he had so much objected. Come high summer, like the recruits in the awkward weight of their full dress, he sometimes felt the heat and the discomfort of his bridle to be intolerable. Yet six year-old Sefton was learning to resign himself to, if not necessarily to live contentedly with, every aspect of cavalry life.

In their eighteenth week the recruits practised riding in the troop formation required on State escorts, alternating with individual demonstrations of the canter. By the end of the nineteenth, heads that had been awkward in the shaking helmets, hands that had felt tortured in those stiff gauntlets, clutching reins in the left hand and sword-hilts close to thighs in the right, began to supple and ease, and even the little finger of the right hand, pulled back behind the sword-hilt to hold the glistening blade upright, a position excruciatingly uncomfortable in the beginning, now passed unnoticed.

'Brought to near perfection on the sand of a Rotten Row dappled by plane-tree shadow.' (Leslie Lane)

With double-rank troop drills brought, in the twentieth week, to perfection, on the sand of a Rotten Row dappled by plane tree shadows, the recruits were ready to be paraded for their final inspection, and so to be fully-blossomed 'mounted dutymen'. Soldiers who, five months before, were gauche youths had become men. Whether or not they appreciated the fact, they had cause to be grateful to Sefton and his kind. In 1969 many a green recruit came to respect that young black gelding with a blaze, four socks and a thoroughbred presence, and to remember, for the rest of their lives, the instructor's refrain: *Ride, ter-rot ... keep your wits about you, that man on Sefton, if you start taking liberties with that horse he'll toss you straight out of the saddle, have a care! ... Look lively now, let's have the jumps in!*

Sefton was perhaps the best tutor, the best character-builder, that some of those young men ever had.

But was he happy? He was cared for round the clock, groomed, watered and fed a substantial, balanced diet; he was exercised (albeit not always as he would have chosen); his stable-mates, with whom he could communicate, right and left, were constantly there; and there was a vet on hand to treat his smallest ailment or injury. His programme was nearly always the same (nothing dull about that, horses love routine). But was there a feeling that his life was unfulfilled, that, with his look of breeding and his superior conformation, he should be destined for higher challenges?

6 A Blues and Royals Horse

While Sefton was teaching recruits to ride during that summer of 1969, the close regimental observer might have pointed out to the visitor one minute man-made difference in the horse's appearance, as distinct from his appearance when he was on Guard during the previous winter. Where his off-fore hoof had carried the regimental number, RHG 61, another letter was added, to make RHG/D 61. Although this meant little to Sefton, it held the greatest significance for the Household Cavalry. That 'D' stood for 'Dragoons'.

It came about like this. For the sake of national economic expediency, a decision was made, in the late 1960s – for at least the fourth time since the end of the Second World War – to reduce the size of the Army. The Royal Armoured Corps had already suffered heavily; they were to suffer again. Regiments with long and glorious histories, such as the 9th and 12th Lancers, the 3rd and 7th Hussars and the 4th and 8th Hussars, had been forged into single units. Further amalgamations must now be effected, the regiments selected for that fate being, once more, those that had never been subjected to a merger before. In the Household Cavalry The Life Guards, having once comprised two regiments, fused as one in 1922, were saved. The Royal Horse Guards (the Blues) were less fortunate, and so, in the Royal Armoured Corps, the Cavalry of the Line, were, among others, the highly distinguished and exclusive 1st Royal Dragoons, known, for short, as the Royals. Neither the Blues nor the Royals had ever been adulterated, so to speak, by juncture with another regiment.

Raised in 1661, the same year as the Blues, the Royals' first assignment was to provide the cavalry for the garrison of Tangier, the North African colony which was part of the Portuguese dowry made to Charles II on his marriage to Catherine of Braganza. Apart from the broad background of three centuries' service as cavalrymen to their Monarch, the Royals shared much with the Blues.

The two regiments had fought together at Sedgmoor in 1685, and in the Seven Years War and the War of the Austrian Succession; they had been comrades-in-arms in the Peninsular campaign and at the Battle of Waterloo; they had shared the tribulations of South Africa and France and Flanders, and they had fought alongside, during the Second World War, in the Desert Army and in the Italian and Normandy campaigns. The Royals, too, had worn the helmet and plume of heavy horsed cavalry; they, too, had a post-war peacekeeping tradition in the armoured car role; they, too, held a distinguished sporting record, especially in the equestrian field; they, too,

eaving Buckingham Palace for a State Opening of Parliament. Sefton is n the right. (Press Association)

were not averse to pomp and circumstance. In short, the Royals enjoyed the esteem of a very smart and stylish regiment.

There is not a unit in the British Army that is not enormously proud of its heritage, that does not feel jealous concerning its own distinctive character, that does not believe it is second to none. If the Blues must amalgamate, they could not have chosen a more suitable partner than the Royals. No regiment of the Line was more eligible to take the status of Household Cavalry. As for the Royals' advantage, elevation into that Corps offered yet higher distinction and a thrilling new dimension.

Before the two regiments were forged together, in April, 1969, to form a new regiment of Household Cavalry – the Blues and Royals (Royal Horse Guards and 1st Dragoons) – the question of which emblems and items of uniform should be retained involved some painful decision-making. For the Royals, becoming a regiment of Household Cavalry meant more sacrifices than it did for the Blues, who were already in that position. The interests of the ceremonial, or public, duties' roles had to take precedence. Consequently, once the amalgamation was effected, the man-in-the-street would not have realised that the image of the Blues had altered. Yet some Royals' embellishments were conceded, the most prominent being their crest. A replica of the copper eagle, which the regiment captured from Napoleon's 105th Regiment at Waterloo, now forms the centre of the Blues and Royals crest, and is worn, in black and gold, by all ranks of the regiment, on the left arm.

For Sefton and the other blacks, life at Wellington Barracks continued precisely as before. When the Royals had had horses, 30 years and more before, they had been bays and browns. Now, like the rest of the Household Cavalry, they would ride blacks or, in the case of their trumpeters, greys, or of their kettle-drummers, skewbalds, piebalds or iron greys. The official abbreviation, RHG/D – Royal Horse Guards/Dragoons – which Sefton wore on his off-fore, seemed strange and rather illogical nomenclature. It was something that was spelt, yet left unspoken. Sefton, for example, was a Blues and Royals horse; no one would have dreamed of referring to him as a Royal Horse Guards/Dragoons horse.

His first new brand, RHG/D 61, still looked very freshly cut on his foot when he was ridden down to camp in August, 1969.

A Blues and Royals division of the Sovereign's Escort for a State Opening of Parliament, showing Sefton on the right of the leading section. 'Some Royals' embellishments were conceded, the most prominent being the replica of the copper eagle which the Royals captured from Napoleon's 105th Regiment at Waterloo, and which is worn, in black and gold, by all ranks, on the left arm.' (Press Association)

7 The Joys of Camping

By late summer, after twenty weeks' riding school, the Queen's Birthday Parade and the annual service at Windsor for the Knights of the Garter (at which the Household Cavalry, dismounted, line the processional route to St George's Chapel) those cavalrymen whom Sefton had helped to fashion were eagerly looking forward to the sojourn of summer camp. Something of a busman's holiday, as well as the climax of their apprenticeship, it took place during August or September.

The Life Guards and the Blues and Royals took it in turn to spend a fortnight at a place called Stoney Castle, between Guildford and Bagshot, on a large open field flanked by the Surrey heathland, while the squadron left behind in London fulfilled all the Queen's Life Guard and other commitments for that fortnight. Camp made a wonderful break for both the men and the horses.

In late July and early August, in order to help get the horses fit for the arduous ride to Stoney Castle, the troops set off once a week or so, in the early morning, down the buzzing, tight-thronged streets and over one of the Thames bridges, for Richmond Park or Hounslow Heath, to the first large expanses of grass that young horses like Sefton had seen since the Melton Mowbray days. Those London horses found the marches quite arduous, and when Sefton returned to his troop stables, he felt fingers searching over his back and round his belly for saddle and girth galls, and round his legs for knocks.

They were exciting excursions for Sefton. For, although it is unlikely that a horse sees things in quite the variety of colours that we do, but rather in shades and nuances, he can sense the brightness of a rural landscape, he can hear the noises of the countryside, the birds, the wind in the trees, and he can distinguish every different odour, especially the delicious and predominating scent of the grass of high summer. There was time, on those occasions, too, for a brief graze, a wonderful diversion, as the only green meal he tasted in his London manger was the occasional ration of lucerne or other cut leaf (not always very fresh), mixed in his dry feed.

Perhaps, on the morning of that 1969 ride to Surrey, Sefton and his young contemporaries sensed that there was something bigger and better in the air than usual. Reveille stables were at 5.30 when London was relatively quiet. Soon a feed bag and a trooper's waterproof were tied to his saddle, a tethering rope lay round his neck and a universal bit was in his mouth. Pervading his troop stables was an air of happy expectancy, quite different from the somewhat ominous atmosphere prevailing, say, on the morning of an escort

Riding down to camp. 'In columns of troops, marching by half-sections and heading towards Staines, via Hounslow.' (Mike Roberts)

A break on the six-hour journey. (Mike Roberts)

rehearsal or the annual inspection by the Major-General commanding the Guards Division.

By 6.30 it was *half-sections right, walk march*! and the Blues and Royals squadron were on the road, upwards of 80 horses and khaki riders in column of troops, marching by half-sections, in pairs, through Chelsea, and heading towards Staines, via Hounslow. A squadron of cavalry had been no rare sight up to 1939. But, 30 years later, few suburban Londoners, or Middlesex folk, had seen such a thing in their lives. Early morning risers, hearing the heralding *clip-clop*, stopped and looked up with obvious pleasure at the stirring sight. Their number might have included one or two veterans who had ridden with a cavalry regiment in the swansong days between the Wars, or who had even trotted into battle. The nostalgia induced by that brave spectacle would certainly have brought a lump to their throats, if not tears of sentiment to their eyes.

As the squadron emerged from Greater London, Sefton noticed gradual changes in the sights, sounds and scents. The traffic was busy on the Great West Road, but he did not really mind traffic any more. Although he objected if a vehicle got too close to him, the roaring, smelly, metal creatures seemed to be mostly bark and little bite. Sometimes the squadron came level with a field containing cows or sheep, whose lowing or bleating was a meaningless language; but once or twice they passed paddocks in which horses grazed and, in the trotting or walking ranks, ears would cock and twitch and a whicker or a neigh would sound, as though to say, 'Hey, you look interesting, so am I!' Sefton and his brother-geldings were no sexless beings.

Following a halt at Bedfont Green, Hounslow, where Sefton and his mates were given their nose-bags and a good long drink of water, they journeyed the last three hours to their Surrey destination without a break.

The green sward of Stoney Castle, the country home of the Household Cavalry for nearly half a century, lies just across the railway from Pirbright Camp, the home of the Guards Depot. There Sefton found himself in scaffolding horse-lines with straw-scattered earth for his floor. All around were stacks of straw and hay bales, beyond them marquees and neat rows of tents, and, beyond those, the wooden pavilion that had served as the officers' mess since the 1920s.

The aroma of new rope and freshly unfolded canvas, mingled with the odours of pine and heather and grass, devoid at last of pollution, were to Sefton and his mates like the smell of an oasis to a desert traveller just in from days on the baking sand-dunes. And what a relief to have the saddle removed from his back and the bit from his mouth, to have his head-collar buckled on and to be led to a trough of water! The temperature was well up in the seventies; Sefton drank deep: he had never carried a man so far in his life.

The trooper who had ridden him led him that afternoon to the long grass by the woods that flanked the camp, and – shades of his Waterford colthood and Melton limbo – let him graze it and roll on it for a quarter of an hour. It was especially satisfying to rub that part of his back that had been subjected to the pressure of saddle and rider, and it was good to feel the dusty earth against his skin. As for the flavour of the grass, he luxuriated in that, too; it was like the proverbial manna from heaven. Although he was not accustomed to grazing, his acute equine sense of taste, heightened in those first four years on Irish pasture, told him exactly what was wholesome and what was bad. When his lips picked up a pebble, or a twig, or some unwanted weed, he would carefully allow it to drop from his mouth while masticating the good stuff.

The horse-lines at Stoney Castle Camp, Surrey. 'The aroma of rope and freshly unfolded canvas, mingled with the odours of pine and heather and grass, devoid at last of pollution, were perhaps to Sefton and his mates, something like the wafts of an oasis to a desert traveller.' (Mike Roberts)

'Over the sandy, undulating Surrey hills.' (Press Association)

During the first couple of days the soldiers received weapon-handling refresher lessons, then they practised on the Pirbright ranges with the sub-machine gun, qualifying as marksmen, or, as the case might be, first or second-class shots, a reminder that the Household Cavalryman is a warrior first and a ceremonial soldier only second. They had received their basic training as infantrymen at the nearby Guards Depot; they could have gone to war within a week.

A few of them were busy, too, repairing the hunter-trial course in the wood at the back of the camp, which had become delapidated since the previous year. As for Sefton and his companions, it was a relief not to be in demand. Feeling rather subdued in the forty-eight hours following that unaccustomed marathon ride, all they wanted was to be led around the field, or to be left alone to recoup their strength. Some of the horses were suffering quite badly from treads on the coronet, and from brushing wounds. But those were soon put right.

Day after day, following that opening interlude, Sefton was ridden out with his troop on map-reading or minor tactical exercises, over the sandy, undulating, pine-and heather-clad Surrey hills. There were steep slopes to climb and descend, and ditches and holes and boulders to be avoided. Few of the horses were as sure-footed as Sefton. As they all put on muscle, so their corn was increased, and so the length of those daily rides was extended. Once they made their way to Tweseldown racecourse and, on another occasion, to the Long Valley, near Aldershot, which had been an arena for cavalry exercises for over a century.

Sometimes, when they came to healthy looking streams, there were halts for a drink and, at the lunch break when saddles were removed, or, at least, girths loosened, there was usually another chance for a graze. When Sefton returned to camp each day he found that far more attention was paid to his feet and legs than usual. Over-reaches, bruised soles, sprained tendons and cuts were treated every day by one of the farriers.

Camp was not all Elysium. Sefton experienced long rides with heavy, sudden downpours, in which he flattened his ears against the lashing rain-needles, obliged to pick his way with great care on the slippery inclines. Nor were those nights of late summer always clear and starlit. Once or twice there were canopies of thundercloud, and he learned the discomfort, on ink-black nights, of standing in a muddy stall, listening to his comrades' neighs of alarm while the storm beat down on their heads and pattered against their waterproof rugs. But the outbursts never lasted long, and next day Sefton's coat would glow again under the health-giving sun. He had never been fitter.

On fine nights, when he stood there, tethered by his halter, he could hear the troopers singing their songs around a camp fire, songs like *The Wild West Show, She'll be Comin' round the Mountain, Tipperary* and that interminable, enigmatic refrain that Household Cavalrymen sing to the tune of *Bless Them All*:

> I am saying goodbye to my horse,
> I am saying goodbye to my horse,
> And when I am saying goodbye to my horse,
> I am saying good-bye to my horse!

The men were in good heart, and that helped to put the horses in good heart, too.

Nearly all the horses took part in the inter-troop jumping competition, and were popped over that small handy-hunter course in the woods behind the camp, with its lane of posts-and-rails, ditches, fallen tree trunks and brush fences to jump, and gates and narrow gaps, which could only be negotiated quickly if the horse stood still, or if he shifted quietly, deftly and obediently, when so required. All this came quite naturally and easily to Sefton. With an instinctive sense of timing, a long reach, the possession of the so-called 'fifth leg' that always had him landing fair and square on difficult places, and the well-bred horse's courage to accompany those assets, he was beginning to earn a new reputation. As a result of all the hard work he had put in, his image was better than it had ever been. He had acquired muscle at the expense of fat, and that was a change for the better.

The Officers and NCOs were taking a closer look at him. They were summing up all those physical points that obviously had not lied: the well-placed scapula and humerus that gave him his fine sloping shoulder, and, with it, his rakish stride and long reach; the broad chest and depth through the heart, the clean legs and flexy pasterns, the well-balanced overall proportions, the close coupling and the swaggering presence; all the quality look that stood him out among his comrades.

There were other contests, events which he may have observed, but in which he did not yet participate: tent pegging, for example, and a sword, lance and revolver competition, in which the riders were required to pierce a dummy with the first two weapons and explode a rubber balloon with the third. Older horses than he, well tried horses that would canter in an unveering straight line, were reserved for those competitions. Would Sefton's turn come?

The adventures of Stoney Castle camp gave him a new self-respect. His bad name as a ceremonial horse was already beginning to fade against his new prowess as an 'athlete'. By the end of those two weeks he was as hard as he had ever been in his life, so that the ride back to Wellington Barracks was a great deal easier than the ride down. In fact it was no trouble at all. He must have felt quite like an old campaigner.

Naturally, the weeks ahead saw him soften again. But Sefton was not fated to a life of eternal riding school. Straight after camp the two Squadron Leaders were called upon to volunteer a few extra horses to add to those serving with the Household Cavalry regiment stationed in the British Army of the Rhine, which was then the Blues and Royals. Sefton's new squadron leader,* recognising him as a horse of considerable potential, if not of immediate reliability, decided that a stint in Germany would mature him. It was to prove the making of him.

* Major The Hon. A.H.G. Broughton (now Lord Fairhaven and a Steward of the Jockey Club)

One of Sefton's friends taking it easy with his rider. Wexford and Trooper Boyd. (Press Association)

8 Proclaimed 'King' in Germany

The horse box proceeded direct from Wellington Barracks to the Dover–Zeebrugge ferry, and next day Sefton, with the half-dozen replacements for duty in Germany who accompanied him, arrived in Lothian Barracks, by the Westphalian town of Detmold. He was rather more exhausted following that journey than he had felt after his road, sea and rail marathon from County Waterford to Leicestershire in 1967. Then, as a minimum, he had enjoyed a change of accommodation, a chance to move around in the cattle lairages at Dun Laoghaire and Holyhead and the boat's cattle pen; whereas on this journey, not only had he suffered the constantly rumbling discomfort of the horse-box during the sea crossing, but he had been in a closely confined position throughout.

At Lothian Barracks, which had been built under Hitler's rule to accommodate a horse artillery regiment, he and his comrades were led into a fine, airy stable block containing 30 ample loose-boxes with vertical bars resting on waist-high boards, and wood chippings for bedding. To Sefton's nose the odours were widely dissimilar from those of the London Barracks – the smell of the building, of the bedding, the whole atmosphere of Germany was quite different. The twelve horses already in residence to greet the new arrivals were mostly fellow-blacks and trumpeters' greys. One or two others, chestnuts and bays, were the private property of individual Officers. Sefton stared at his neighbours and pawed his bedding, gently and tentatively pushed his nostrils against the bars, giving and receiving silent messages, gauging the others' natures. Next morning, outside the stables, everything seemed just as strange.

When we speak of service with the Blues and Royals as such we imply the operational regiment, which means armoured cars at Windsor, and tanks or armoured cars abroad. Since the late 1960s the regiment has interchanged with The Life Guards between the Household Cavalry's home station, Windsor, and the British Army of the Rhine, the regiment at Windsor often serving stints in Northern Ireland or having squadrons on detachment in Cyprus or on training elsewhere overseas. The Blues and Royals had amalgamated at Detmold earlier in 1969, the year that Sefton was posted there.

When he was ridden out on exercise in the morning he found the surroundings most bizarre. His senses were assailed by the vibrations and rumbles of Chieftain tank tracks, the drone of scout car engines, the occasional whine of high frequency radio sets, and by the reek of oil and grease. Here turret guns and automatic small arms took the place of ceremonial swords. This was a place where the cavalryman strode about his business, not in helmet and cuirass, but in tank suit, or denim overalls, or wearing a business-like khaki pullover, encircled with the blue-and-red striped canvas stable belt of the Household troops, and a beret with the badge that bore the Royal emblem E II R, surrounded by a ring inscribed with the words 'the Blues and Royals'.

The Blues and Royals were in the 20th Armoured Brigade of the 1st British Corps. They comprised a brilliantly oiled cog in the wheel of the front-line troops of the North Atlantic Treaty Organisation, a highly professional unit, forever on emergency call, training interminably to maintain the highest standards of battle efficiency. Yet, being Household Cavalry, the regiment had to be ever mindful of its responsibility to its Mounted Squadron in London, its shop front, its first pride and delight.

Household Cavalrymen were then, as they are today, probably the most versatile soldiers in the world. Not only are they proficient in the tank and armoured car tactics and trades; not only do they provide paratroopers and pilots, Special Air Service troopers and mountain warfare specialists; but most of them are interchangeable, too, in their operational and equestrian-ceremonial roles. Following from this a subtle distinction may be detected

The late Captain R.C. Wilkinson on Sefton in 1970. 'An officer who possessed an unusual intuition about horses, and for whom horses always went well.'

between the bearing and air of the standard Household Cavalryman and, for example, his counterpart in the regiments of the Royal Armoured Corps. Apart from the fact that the Household Cavalryman must be taller, those of them who have trained with the ilk of Sefton and have been through spells of mounted duty show a superior, yet indefinable, loose-limbed poise and confidence which, it must be admitted, most men in the line regiments lack. Even the humblest trooper has learned to control and command another living being, a horse, with all the character-building advantages which that experience entails.

But a large element of those who belonged to the service regiment, having originally volunteered for tanks and armoured cars, had never put in a tour of duty with the horses. So that was the *raison d'être* of Sefton and his stable-mates at Detmold. The dozen-and-a-half horses were there – some, like Sefton, dismissed from London either in disgrace or on remand – to initiate aspirants for the regiment's Mounted Squadron, to start them off with a lead when they reached London, not undergoing the full twenty weeks' school, but striking off a ride or two ahead of the recruits who were posted direct for mounted duty following their basic military training at the Guards Depot. The Household Cavalry regiment stationed in Germany also ran Rhine Army equitation courses.

So riding school was Sefton's first mission and riding school at Detmold was his routine employment for the next five years of his life. And he had forgotten nothing. He was not everyone's favourite, he would never be the choice of the feeble or the faint-hearted; he was famous for his reaction to the feel of an indolent or careless soldier in his saddle, or one who was not quite as kind and easy on his mouth as he would have liked. Such men would still be dumped on the tan.

(Above): *Captain Wilkinson competing for the Booth-Jones Trophy on Sefton. They won the Cup in 1970.* (Below): *At a meet of the Weser Vale Hounds during the 1969–70 season. Sefton (Captain Wilkinson up) is on the right.*

Captain Christopher Haworth-Booth, The Life Guards, Master of Bloodhounds, with his hunter, Sefton. 'I could not have chosen a more congenial companion,' he admitted, 'he was willing, even-tempered and long suffering.'

The trainee rides were not continuous and, at the time Sefton reached the barracks, there was a lull. Consequently he was available for recreational purposes. At least one man in the Blues and Royals had discovered his potential: Captain R.C. Wilkinson, the Regimental Signals Officer and Assistant Adjutant, who had been with the Blues Mounted Squadron during Sefton's apprenticeship. Captain Wilkinson was a dedicated horseman and, albeit no lightweight, he was an officer who had an unusual intuition about horses and for whom horses always went well.

There were two hunter trials on the programme that autumn, the first to be organised by the 14th/20th Hussars and the second by the 16th/5th Lancers. Captain Wilkinson was determined to try Sefton in both.

Most tragically, Richard Wilkinson (who was described by his obituarist, Lieutenant-Colonel Parker Bowles, as 'a marvellous officer, gentleman and friend'*) died towards the end of 1981, while taking part in a regimental run in Windsor Great Park. (He was then aged 37 and second-in-command of the Blues and Royals). It is therefore not possible to give a first-hand report of his relationship with Sefton. However, we may imagine him taking out the six-year-old black with the broad white blaze and the four white socks, sometimes in the afternoon, sometimes early in the morning before parade, and always on Saturdays; getting him fit, starting with an hour's work, building up to two hours, trotting him up and down the slopes, schooling him over jumps, gradually heightening his performance.

The courses were some 2,500 metres long, including about 20 obstacles, brush fences and poles, fallen trees, stacked railway sleepers and sheep hurdles, simulated stiles and level crossings. When the big days came, Sefton was as calm and nonchalant as it was always his nature to be on those occasions. He pricked forward his ears, went determinedly, but carefully and wisely, at each jump, to leap it like a stag. On both occasions he carried Captain Wilkinson in to win the first of a great many prize monies that would be due to him, Sefton, over the years. From having been regarded, only the summer before, as something of a liability, a bit of a joke, he was now a 'blue-eyed boy'. To endorse his new reputation, during the following summer he won the Rhine Army Cup with Captain G.H. Tweedie, Blues and Royals, in the saddle, at Bad Lippspringe. That made him a champion.

Captain Wilkinson was instrumental, in 1969, in forming the regiment's private hunt, called the Weser Vale, and as Sefton was to play a leading role, a most valued and integral part in that recreation, it is worthwhile to sketch the heritage of the hunt.

The hunting of wild animals with hounds has not been permitted in the Federal Republic during the past half century. During the 1920s, the first German socialist government, regarding it as a symbol of the despotic power of the landlords, imposed as much restriction on such field sports as they could, and that kind of hunting was banned, in the 1930s, by the Nazi regime. So hunting men and women of the Third Reich and their successors were reduced to following a drag, riding to hounds scenting an aniseed trail.

One of the secrets of the success of the British regimental system is that the officers of each regiment are cast in much the same mould, with similar interests and concepts of amusement, a tradition that helps to create a homogeneous and harmonious fraternity. The officers of the Household Cavalry are preoccupied with polo, steeplechasing and other equestrian activities, game shooting, sailing and skiing, and, perhaps most universally of all, hunting. Of all regiments, the Blues and Royals probably hold the

* *Guards Magazine*, Winter 1981–82.

record for the number of Masters of Hounds who, at one time or another, have served with them.

The story of the Weser Vale hunt begins when the Royal Horse Guards (the Blues) were stationed in Westphalia with the Army of Occupation in the late 1940s, a time when the ban on the hunting of live quarries imposed by the Third Reich was null and void, when the law was the law of the Allies. The regiment was busy with armoured cars, patrolling the East German frontier. Enrolling the help of a number of past officers, who were by then Masters of Hounds in Britain, a group of enthusiasts assembled a motley pack to hunt the hare.

During the regiment's second tour with the Army of the Rhine, in the early 1960s, when the German legislation on live quarry was once more enforced, many Blues spent their Saturday afternoons riding with one of the five German drag packs, which followed a set and predictable course and whose supporters were much preoccupied, in the teutonic tradition, with putting on buttonholes, drinking *schnapps* and indulging in much *bonhomie* at the checks, or rest-places, and at the close of the day.

The determination not to be denied their hunting, simply because they were away from Britain, remained strong. Faced with a third stint of duty in Westphalia, in 1969, Captain Wilkinson and his friends hit upon the idea of bloodhounds in pursuit of a human quarry, the quarry being a member of the regiment who would be given a general direction in which to run, designed to provide the most enjoyable cross-country riding for the followers. In contrast to the rigid certainty of aniseed and animal urine trails, the blood-hounds would be seen to work out their line 'clean boot', as it is called – that is, not from anything carried by the man but from the human scent itself, a rather more exciting diversion.

Securing drafts of hounds from the Masters of the Peak and North Warwickshire packs and also from a Dutch Master of bloodhounds, the co-founders of the Weser Vale hunt staged their opening meet on September 1, 1969, with a fine afternoon's sport, divided into three 'quarry hunts', each of them being about two miles long with ten or so timber obstacles and walls to jump. And this enjoyable ritual was repeated, Saturday after Saturday, from October until early April. Sefton, with Captain Wilkinson in the saddle, was quickly in the lead, soon securing a name for himself as a very useful hunter.

By the time I rode with these hounds, eighteen months later, the Weser Vale had attracted around 20 German horsemen and women, besides a host of Westphalian car and foot followers. I remember a happy, carefree cavalcade riding down to the start of the course where a Corporal-of-Horse laid hounds onto the smell, consisting of a piece of rag which had been regularly handled by the quarry during the previous week. The trooper who played the part of the quarry was already running a field or two ahead. The British, mostly riding the Household Cavalry blacks, wore either their traditional pink, with top hats (hunt staff, velvet caps) and white breeches, or 'ratcatcher' and bowler hats, while the Germans, in scarlet, too, donned their habitual white collars and ties with scarlet coats and velvet caps.

There was a great air of *entente* about the occasion, and I was told that the

The 'quarry' with the last hound to greet him when the author rode with the Weser Vale Bloodhounds in 1971. Captain Haworth-Booth, riding Sefton (right), leads the field.

Weser Vale had done much to foster the growing warmth between the Army and local inhabitants, and even that Rhine Army formation commanders, weary of complaints of damage by German farmers and others, had gone so far as to send for the Weser Vale to run their lines in scarred manoeuvre areas, and that, when the hunt spent the afternoon there, harmony was soon restored. The Household Cavalry horses were, and are, a *sine qua non*, and due credit must go to the remount riders who have schooled them so well as to make them cross-country merchants as well as ceremonial horses. My photograph shows Sefton leading in the field at the last quarry hunt on an occasion when I was out with the Weser Vale in April, 1971.

After Captain Wilkinson left Germany to become Adjutant of the Mounted Regiment, Sefton was promptly adopted by an officer of The Life Guards squadron then temporarily under command of the Blues and Royals. This was Captain C.N. Haworth-Booth, who is riding him in that photograph. Later in 1971 The Life Guards took over at Detmold *en bloc* on a routine posting, from the Blues and Royals, and Captain Haworth-Booth (a former Master, incidentally, of the Eton College Beagles) was appointed joint-Master and huntsman of the Weser Vale. Here is a part of the memoir which he wrote for me of his first encounter with, and impressions of, Sefton:

> When I first reached Detmold and was walking through the stables I singled out from the other horses this well-built one called Sefton, with a

> white face and an odd eye. Now a lot of people attach great significance to the eye of a horse and regard it as a sound guide to his reliability, and it must be admitted, by even his best friends, that Sefton's eye is not his most attractive feature. It is not a sunken or piggy eye, which might denote a sulky temperament, it is just that it is not his best feature. It shows too much white . . .

But Captain Haworth-Booth was not to be put off by that:

> Having ridden him a few times with the Weser Vale I realised that he was a thoroughly reliable horse, and since he did not seem to be anyone's particular favourite, I did not have to exert much pressure in having him allocated to me when the time came, in my role as huntsman of the Bloodhounds. As it turned out I could not have chosen a more congenial companion. He was willing, even-tempered and long suffering. I cannot remember ever having to give him any more guidance than one would give a bicycle. He would always go at the pace I wanted, he could stop and stand rock still – a most valuable and underrated quality in any hunter – and could produce a reasonable turn of speed. He could open a gate, he could jump a gate, and I think, had he been asked to do so, he could have reversed up to a gate and pushed it over . . .

Absolute dependability seemed to be the keynote to Sefton's character. What a contrast to those anxious days of 1968 in London! Captain Haworth-Booth goes on:

> I don't think he developed any particular affinity with the bloodhounds. He simply accepted them (perhaps with a shrug). He took no more notice of them than he took of cars or people, so that I could devote my entire attention to my hounds. This was no small problem out on hound exercise in Germany where the inhabitants just do not expect to see a horse on the road, let alone a mad Englishman on its back, with anything up to 20 dogs grouped round him. Sefton took it all in his stride and he never appeared to experience a moment's anxiety.
>
> He was by no means a lazy horse, but he never did more than was necessary, which meant that he saved his energy, he was economical in his exertions. He had a phlegmatic character, quite unlike those all-too-familiar mounts who are always throwing their heads about and marking time at the double. He never got excited or sweated up, he was a real cool hand. He jumped anything that came his way and had the sense to keep himself and his rider out of trouble. He never ever thought of refusing, and he seemed to take a secret delight in negotiating some particularly big or awkward obstacle, and pretending that he had hardly noticed it . . . I hope that when his time comes St Peter will have the gate open for him. If he doesn't, Sefton will jump it anyway.

Captain Haworth-Booth remembers Sefton as the most respected character in those stables at Detmold, 'so much so that he became known as "the King" by the stable staff . . . he was never sick and hardly ever sorry . . .'

The same couple when Captain Haworth-Booth was Master. 'I hope that, when his time comes,' he said, 'St Peter will have the gate open for him. If he doesn't Sefton will jump it anyway!'

But of course all that rigorous and hazardous work for popular Sefton – alias 'the King' – implied more attention to his needs. He was fed more oats and nuts, he was given boiled feeds after hunting, he had a dose of Epsom once a week to keep his kidneys right, and, once or twice in the season, a physic. His least sign of mud fever was washed with antiseptic; his legs were bandaged against the damp; his scratches were treated with antiseptic solution and wound powder; a careful watch was kept on his tendons, and when he was badly cut the vet was there in double quick time.

When Captain Haworth-Booth gave up the Mastership of the Weser Vale his friends and followers offered him a leaving present. They suggested an equestrian oil portrait of himself, clad, of course, in his huntsman's scarlet, with his bloodhounds. 'Thank you very much,' said Captain Haworth-Booth, 'but I would rather not feature in the picture myself. Could it be simply of

Parading with the hounds at the Rhine Army Summer Show in the early 1970s.

Sefton and my two favourite hounds, Charity and Chary?' So 'the King' was once more in the limelight.

If not actually overworked between 1970 and 1974, Sefton was often stretched close to the limit of his endurance. As the records show, he won prize money for places gained in jumping and hunter trials at nearly all the shows in each of those years during the summer, and was hunted regularly all through the winter months.

How did he behave in the stable? Corporal-Major (then Corporal) Dick Batey, of The Life Guards, was in charge there during most of Sefton's Rhine Army sojourn. He remembers him well:

> Sefton had no stall vices except for laying his ears back when he was being saddled up or having his rug straightened. He looked threatening, but only nipped once to my knowledge. Trooper McGlade was being a little sloppy and kissing Sefton on the nose. Sefton decided on the passionate return and bit him clean through his bottom lip, which had to be stitched . . .

By no means everyone shared Sefton's sense of fun! But what of riding school, the purpose for which he was sent to Germany? Did Sefton's more glamorous activities excuse him that? They did not. Riding school was his habitual work; hunter trials, show jumping and hunting were his diversions. Corporal-Major Batey again:

> On the trainees' rides Sefton was the one to provide the laughs. The trainees, on their first morning, would be allocated horses. The first ten minutes would generally be spent at the walk. When the order for the trot was given, the eyes of the instructors would be fixed on Sefton. For we knew that, as soon as that horse realised he had a novice on his back, he would endeavour to produce a little light entertainment. A few paces into the trot would result in a mischievous equine squeal, a sharp buck and one young rider becoming an expert on air travel and the art of crash landing on the tan. But laughs aside, he was a good school horse . . .

Inimitable Sefton! He might be as quiet and obedient as a puppet in the hunting-field, but there were times, too, when he could not resist giving vent to his humour. Longsuffering, uncomplaining Sefton! Too many of those keen regimental equestrians wanted, show season after show season, hunting season after hunting season, to have a go on 'the King'. Consequently the end of 1974 saw him broken down with strained tendons. 'As a result of which,' Corporal-Major Batey remembers, 'he was blistered and turned out to rest, which, I am pleased to say, did the trick.'

But he was ten years old now. It was decided that the time had come to end his exile, to return him to London.

9 Glamorous Knightsbridge

Following his journey of seventeen hours from Detmold, including five on the Zeebrugge–Dover ferry, Sefton clambered down the horsebox ramp to be led round the yard for fifteen minutes, to stretch his tired, stiff legs, especially those foreleg tendons, strong as steel, but now something of a liability. His surroundings were as unfamiliar to him as the German barracks had been in 1969. For, as you can see from the wall plaque that faces the Park, the barracks at Knightsbridge were completed less than five years before, Sefton's previous London experience having been confined to Wellington:

This Plaque was unveiled by
Field-Marshal Sir Gerald Templer KG and
Admiral of the Fleet Earl Mountbatten of Burma KG
to mark the opening of Hyde Park Barracks on
the 22nd October, 1970

The prefabricated stables at Wellington, next to Buckingham Palace, where Sefton had spent those two bittersweet years of his youth, were long demolished, and the white barracks would soon be restored to house the Foot Guards, their true heirs. Knightsbridge was the Household Cavalry's Number One traditional home. The Hyde Park site, 440 yards long but constrictingly narrow, sandwiched as it is between the Kensington Road and the Park, contrives to pack in up to 450 soldiers, 250 horses and 130 families, not to mention a capacious riding school, a gymnasium and children's kindergarten.

In the old barracks (which had been built for the Household Cavalry of a Queen Empress who ruled over a high proportion of the world's surface – over some 120 million people – and which were demolished during Sefton's sojourn at Wellington) the men had lived above their squadron stables on both sides of a lengthy regimental yard, The Life Guards at the Hyde Park Corner end and the Blues at the Kensington end. But modern hygiene insisting that it was inadvisable to have men sleeping above horses, in the new Elizabethan barracks the small troop rooms, three or four men to each, were all concentrated on the Knightsbridge side, while the stables were erected in two tiers, facing Hyde Park, The Life Guards below and the Blues and Royals above. Sefton now stepped up a concrete ramp to join his troop on the higher level.

Mucking out had its own streamlined labour-saving aspect. Cutting out the old work of forks and wheelbarrows, the mucked bedding was passed by chutes through each troop's stable floor into the rail-held trollies, and thence

Looking towards the Main Gate at Hyde Park Barracks as the Old Guard returns from Whitehall. Sefton is nearest the camera in the second half-section. (Leslie Lane)

onto the trucks sent down by the manure contractors. Here at the new harsh-lined, concrete barracks, too, were built-in hot-feed boiler rooms and underground forage pits, while Sefton experienced, for the first time in his life, the convenience of automatic manger watering.

Notwithstanding such lavish amenity, veterans protested that the accommodation was too much broken down into petty space. They sighed with nostalgia for Queen Victoria's edifice, with its regimentally communal layout, its big troop barrack rooms and the daylight that streamed through the high stable windows. Too much electric glare might be one of Sefton's complaints if he could tell us his minor woes.

Old hands looked askance at him. He had returned with a fresh reputation. He had made a name for himself in the show ring and the hunting-field, with the Army of the Rhine. There was a new style about him, a new air of confidence, a new elegance. All well and good. But 'handsome is . . .' when it comes to ceremonial at Knightsbridge, they said. This was the quadruped who had shamed the 1968 Trooping, who had tipped Corporal-of-Horse Stamford out of the saddle on Queen's Life Guard. This was the one whose diversion it was – unless you were on the *cave* – to nip whatever portion of your anatomy you allowed to be in range of his lethal incisors.

Never mind his long white stockings and his broad white face, but beware that ominous ring of white that shows on his eye! He used to jib at the State bit, remember? Well, he'll probably be back doing the only military thing he's any good at, showing the recruits his paces round the school . . .

Sefton proved such prophets wrong. Major and Riding Master Jackson*, an officer whose appointment dated from 1967 and who had therefore known the new arrival since his raw remount days, was the man to whom the decision on Sefton's next destiny was delegated. Although he was on the tan next day, it was with a different future in mind. He was trotted round the school for half an hour with a State bit on his jaw and for this he showed the utmost disdain. He threw it up and down behind his teeth a couple of times, and then conveyed to his instructor that he did not mind at all. He had been bitted with one instrument or another for seven years, his bars had hardened

* Promoted Lieutenant-Colonel and Riding Master 1980.

(Opposite, above): *The view during the Edwardian era down Knightsbridge from Prince's Gate, showing the old Barracks, which served the Household Cavalry until 1965. (BBC Hulton Picture Library).* (Opposite, below): *The same view today. (Mike Roberts)*

with usage and age. A set of tack was altered and adjusted to fit him precisely, and, within three weeks, for the first time since his youth, his name was down on Squadron Daily Orders for Queen's Life Guard.

His mane and tail were pulled and trimmed and soaped and rinsed, and he endured grooming sessions three times as long as he had experienced in Germany, as any he had known since his Wellington Barracks tyro days. He looked much more the part now in his sheepskin covered saddle, bright-chain and brass headstall and crested curb bit, than he had ever done in 1968. His carriage was splendid, worthy of transporting a general, cocked-hat, to parade, or straight out of a cavalier painting.

He always was and always would be a horse who was not to be neglected with impunity. As the Master's horse, the competition star and the winner of many *deutschmarks* at the shows in Germany, he had become accustomed to adulation. So why should he be treated as run-of-the-mill here in London? One of his methods of attracting notice was to get his teeth into his bridle, when it hung on the stable hook, and to pull it with a dismal clatter to the floor. And since the regimental bridle, or 'head kit', takes a good deal of cleaning, polishing and arranging in a uniform pattern, that habit imposed quite a test on his dutyman's humour and patience.

He was put down for Guard, week in week out – to make a journey that was partially new to him, down Hyde Park's South Carriageway, through Hyde Park Corner, down tree-lined Constitution Hill (with his trooper bringing his sword from the 'slope' to the 'carry' and giving an 'eyes right' at the Palace), and so from the broad, rosy Mall, which had first resounded to the

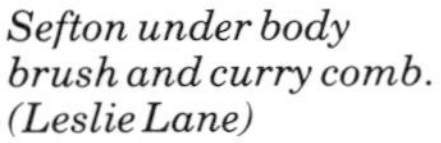

Sefton under body brush and curry comb. (Leslie Lane)

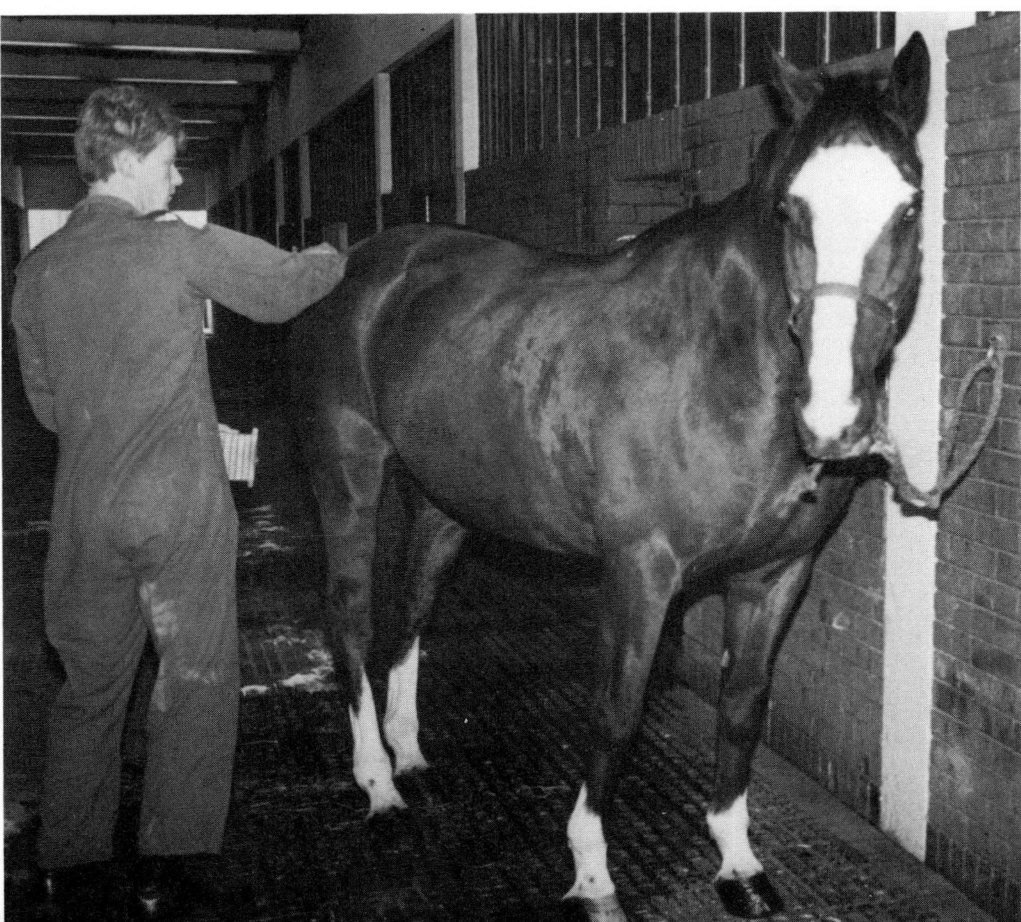

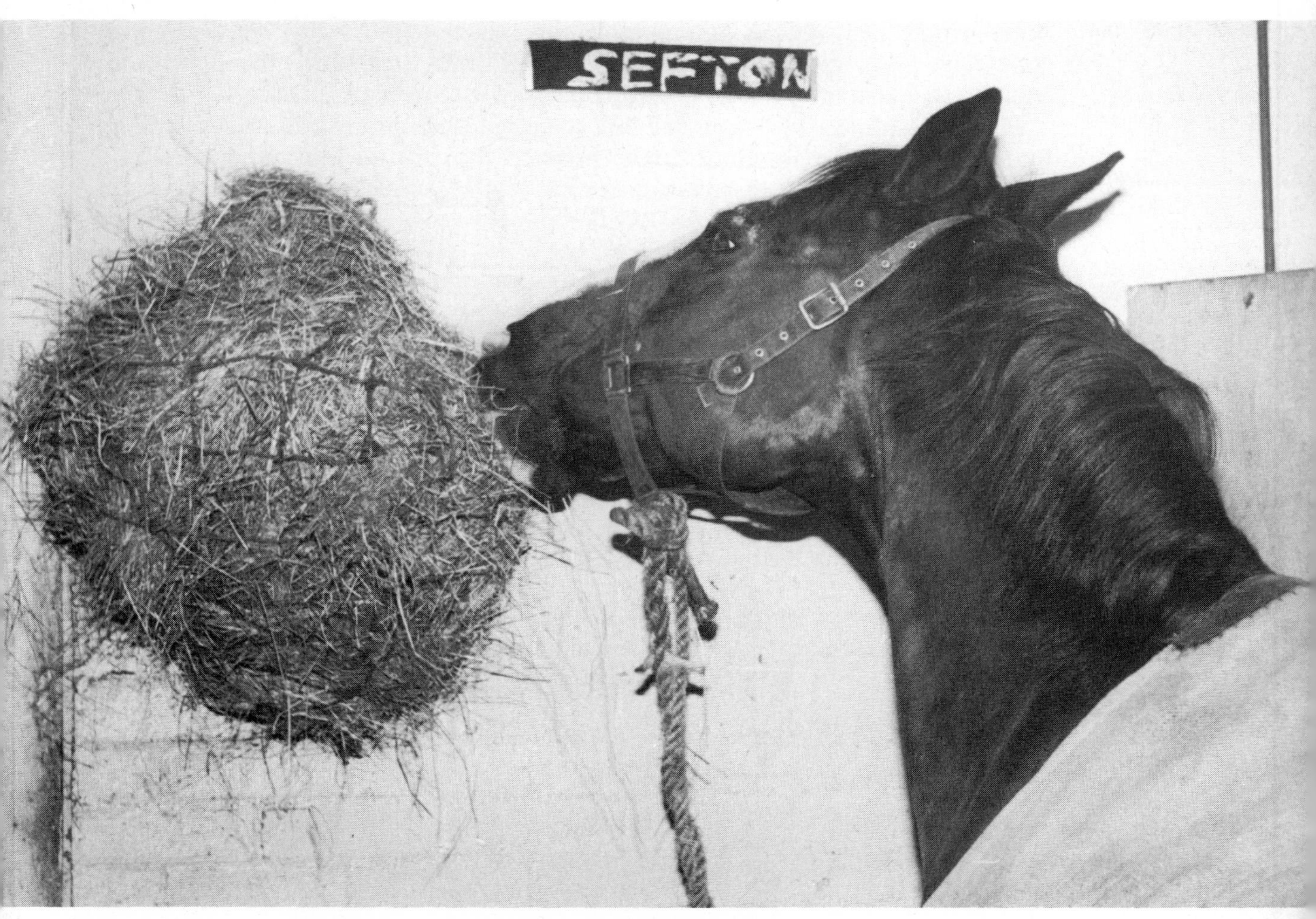

A bite of hay. (Leslie Lane)

sound of Sefton's shoes on the occasion of the 1968 Birthday Parade, to the Horse Guards forecourt and those ancient Guard stables.

Fortunate the trooper who was allotted him. For Sefton was a horse with whom you could quite easily be awarded a Whitehall sentry box, if you were up to his standard, and a box was something that members of the Queen's Life Guard would give a lot of time and trouble to secure.

A horse's sense of observation is exceedingly acute; in particular, nothing, it seems, ever escaped Sefton's notice. Given his renowned showmanship, he surely relished facing onto Whitehall, with that busy street to keep his senses occupied, not so much with the maelstrom of traffic – to the frantic flash and roar of which the nerves of older London horses soon became nearly immune – but with the passers-by stopping to admire him, tourists, pedestrian commuters and City visitors (although, it should be added, they are requested not to do so) pushing biscuits and sugar lumps and slices of carrot and some not-so-welcome titbits up to his condescending mouth. Or holding up their infants to stroke his white nose and saying, 'Isn't he lovely,' or 'Ooh, what a nice old face this one's got, but mind, dearie, he's not a toy,

Passing Buckingham Palace: 'Eyes left!' Sefton is nearest the camera (Mike Roberts)

he'll have your paws for supper.' All good distraction so far as Sefton was concerned.

In stark contrast to his hunting and showing seasons and interminable riding school in faraway Westphalia, he spent many, many hours, in the late '70s and early '80s, on Sovereign's (and other) escorts, or on rehearsals for those pageant occasions: in 1975 for the State visit of the King of Sweden; in 1976 for the President of Tanzania; in 1977 for the Silver Jubilee; in 1978 for the President of Portugal; in 1979 for the President of Kenya; in 1980 for the King of Nepal; in 1981 for the President of Nigeria, not to mention the Royal Wedding; in 1982 for the Sultan of Oman; and during each year for the perennial State Opening of Parliament and the Queen's Birthday Parade, in which Sefton stood out, not as a maverick, as he had done in the previous decade, but, with his new presence and obedience, as the very model of cavalry pomp and circumstance.

Each year, at the start of what London's army calls the ceremonial season, Sefton and his mates and their riders go through six weeks of troop and squadron drills over the yielding earth of Hyde Park's Rotten Row, finishing the programme with two regimental drills, the first in khaki, topped by a helmet, the second in full dress. And there again was the Riding Master, Major Jackson, who held the responsibility for the equitation training of every man present, and the remount training of every horse present, trotting up and down the line putting everything to rights.

Sefton has a name for being a comfortable trotting horse, and since Household Cavalrymen do not rise in the saddle when trotting on parade, a smooth and easy trot, a trot that does not jolt the rider, a 'good sit-down' as the jargon has it, is a heavensent equine quality. He was at once a showman and a 'lovely sit-down'.

With this vision of the new Sefton in the mind's eye – swaggering out of the barracks at Knightsbridge, one of perhaps 170 or 180 horses and soldiers in full panoply, brave and bright and stirring as the legions spilling from the gates of Rome, let us now focus on him as a participant in the two greatest London ceremonies of recent years.

His troop stables. (Leslie Lane)

10 Royal Occasions *Par Excellence*

1977. Silver Jubilee Year was well underway by the middle of May, and Sefton and his friends were destined for some novel tourism. Now they were on their way by horsebox to Glasgow, where they were taken into cattle pens, adjacent to the docks. Their riders, who were living in the pens, too, were there to greet them, having travelled by train; and rarely in the history of Household Cavalry ceremonial had the soldiers been called upon to groom and polish and dress in such squalid conditions, with cleaning kits and full dress and saddlery having to be carefully preserved from the strawdust and grime.

During the next few days they exercised along the City's streets, preparing for their part in 1977's first great morning. When the Royal train drew into Glasgow Central, they escorted the Queen and the Duke of Edinburgh on their State drive. 200,000 people lined the streets to applaud.

With that task behind them they were loaded once more onto the fleet of horseboxes, packed like bottles in crates, cramped but secure, heading north-east for Redford Barracks, Edinburgh, where they were saddled at 4 am next morning – and four out of the next six mornings as well: for a Sovereign's Escort on the State drive to the Palace of Holyroodhouse; for a Captain's Escort for the service of the Order of the Thistle and the installation of the Prince of Wales as a Knight of the Order; and, finally, from St Giles Cathedral, providing another Escort for the opening of the General Assembly of the Church of Scotland, and for the Queen's return to Holyroodhouse. Then the black horses made their exit up the grassy slope past Arthur's Seat, behind the Castle and back to Barracks. Sefton bore a full-dress trooper for six hours that day, mostly standing still. But that was not much trouble for a veteran of his confidence.

He had not returned more than a day or two to Knightsbridge when he felt a body brush swept powerfully across his flanks for yet another hour, the saddle and sheepskin over his spine, the once dreaded State curb in his mouth. Then he was lined up on the barrack square and ridden down to Whitehall for Guard again. And what a programme ensued.

June 7, Jubilee Day – 'The Big Day,' remarked Captain Walker-Okeover, a Blues and Royals officer who took part. 'We had slightly over 200 horses on parade, which was more than anyone could remember, and the yard at Knightsbridge was completely filled with the black beasts.'* For the journey to the Service of Thanksgiving in St Paul's Cathedral, the Household

* *Guards Magazine*, Silver Jubilee Number

Cavalry found escorts for the Queen and the Duke, the Queen Mother and other members of the Royal Family. The processional route was bright with flags and banners and every pavement, every window thronged to capacity with happy people.

The last Saturday in May and the first in June were devoted to rehearsals for Trooping the Colour, which took place before the Queen on June 11. Jubilee fervour was still at its height. Her Majesty's sidesaddle approach down the Mall was heralded by a breathless hush, then a murmuring crescendo, accompanied by the fluttering of a galaxy of Union Jacks like thousands of little waves on a choppy ocean, then a mighty roar of popularity. In 1968 Sefton would have gone half crazy with alarm, now he was as cool as they come. May we assume that, for him, all this noise was just reflected glory?

Another morning in the third week of June saw him onto a horsebox again, on duty for the Royal visit to Wales, and that night and the next in temporary stables at Maindy barracks, Cardiff. The people of Scotland and Wales, unlike Londoners, were unaccustomed to the jingling, flashing splendour and immaculately trained hoofbeats of the Household Cavalry. Their impression had been nothing more than a minuscule television screen picture, from which it was not possible to feel the full visual and aural impact of a State drive. That was partly why the citizens of Glasgow and Edinburgh and Cardiff, in particular, were so full of breathless anticipation, so charged with admiration when their Queen, the pinnacle of the pyramid of State,

In London's shop window: Sefton on sentry duty. (Mike Roberts)

passed by.

Those cavalry escorts were the embodiment of Royal guardianship. Up to a century and a half previously – that was before the foundation of the police – the Household Cavalry had, in every way, been the protectors of their Monarch. Although their role was now essentially ceremonial, the symbols of cuirass and helmet and sword, of the equine mobility given by Sefton and his like, and of the colourful inspiration of cavalry *en masse*, moved as the first metaphor of Britain's determination, come what may, to maintain her Monarchy in the traditional style.

Who would want to harm the Sovereign or members of her family? Every era has thrown up its attackers of Royalty. Charles the Second escaped the regicides of the Rye House Plot, Queen Victoria avoided the bullet that was aimed at her by a lunatic in the crowd as she passed him in her coach; in 1981, Queen Elizabeth's horse danced across the road when a young man fired blanks at her while she rode down the Mall for her Birthday Parade. She was wearing no protective headgear; she might have been thrown. There is little the ceremonial soldier can do to counter such assault. Even with a stalwart such as Sefton for his mount he cannot hope to be much more than a token of Her Majesty's pricelessness, or, by paradox, perhaps, of her personal courage, of her willingness to travel exposed along the crowd-lined streets in this age of bombs and assassins.

July 28, 1981. About 10.30 pm. See Sefton and his fellows dozing on their straw in Hyde Park Barracks, half wakened by unusual noises, *pop, crackle, bang*; and, with the noises, flashes penetrating the stables' apertures, brightening their dimmed electric light. The sky above the Park was decorated with multi-coloured sparks, with firework patterns to celebrate the wedding the next day of the Prince of Wales to Lady Diana Spencer. It was not long before the display was over and the horses resigned themselves to the habitual background sound of the traffic on the South Carriageway. But that festivity heralded for Sefton another early *reveille*.

July 29. The eyes of the whole world were on the bride and bridegroom and the pageantry surrounding them. Never in the annals of London, not even in Jubilee year, had such crowds been recorded, as gathered to share that Royal day. Never had the outside world taken a closer interest in a British event. Through television sets in the Eastern hemisphere, as well as the West, Sefton and his mates were projected into city and shanty town, castle and tenement, factory and farmhouse, drawing room and timber shack, the wide world over.

Few, if any, shared that day as closely as the Queen's Guards. And none with greater glamour than the 'blacks' of Knightsbridge, Sefton prominently among them, trotting sedately to St Paul's and back to the Palace, and from there over Westminster Bridge to Waterloo station, to see the nation's dearly fêted couple – with a bunch of 20 blue and silver balloons marked 'Just married' on the back of their State landau – onto the railway leg of their honeymoon.

'We all have our memories of the day,' enthused Major De Ritter, of The Life Guards, who commanded one of the escorts. 'The millions of flags,

The Prince and Princess of Wales on their wedding day. The Princess and Lieutenant-Colonel Parker Bowles, Field Officer of the Escort, exchange smiles. The officer riding next to Prince Charles is Captain N. Hadden-Paton, also Blues and Royals. (The Sun)

klaxon horns, church bells, euphoric cheering, confetti, rice and a sea of smiling faces, all of which had the effect of "turbo charging" the horses. Suffice it to say that all 170 horses went there and back safely.'* Nor can the Prince and Princess have forgotten the horses in their message of thanks: 'Please convey our warmest congratulations to all those of the Household Division concerned in today's ceremony for the superb way in which they performed their duties. They helped tremendously to make our wedding such a happy and memorable event. Charles and Diana.'

Come August each year Sefton and the others were ridden down for three weeks to the scaffolding lines at Stoney Castle Camp, in Surrey, with the canopy of the stars for their ceiling, and long troop rides across the hills of Pirbright and Aldershot. He did not camp only with his squadron, as he had done in the late 1960s, but (while the King's Troop of the Royal Horse Artillery stood in to mount the Queen's Life Guard from their barracks at St John's Wood) he journeyed with the whole of the Mounted Regiment, a procedure that was begun in 1972. There he excelled in those competition events, jumping and handy hunter, through which he had first caught the eye of the cognoscenti as a rather green six-year-old, and by which he achieved such fame in Germany.

He was now in busy demand for two other sports: skill-at-arms – sword,

* *Guards Magazine*, Autumn, 1981

The Life Guards in Escort Formation. (Mike Roberts)

The Queen's coach passing through Horse Guards forecourt following a State Opening of Parliament, with the Queen's Life Guard, mounted by The Life Guards, turned out to salute her. (Mike Roberts)

lance and revolver – and tent pegging. For the uninitiated the sword, lance and revolver test involves the piercing of dummies, first with a sword, then with a lance, and, lastly, bursting a rubber balloon with a pistol, all in a brief space of time. In tentpegging the competitor gallops towards a series of pegs driven into the ground, and endeavours to lift them out with the point of his lance.

At the Regiment's Open Day, which is staged on the last Sunday of camp, there is one contest for junior NCOs and troopers and one for seniors, in each of those two events. Old Sefton, being a straight galloping, unflinching and totally manageable horse, of a very special calibre, was more often than not ridden in both classes of both events. And year after year, when the Royal Tournament and the Royal Windsor Horse Show came round, he was a regular favourite of the experts.

He was cast, too, in an even more important performance. Who calls himself a true Britisher and is not familiar with the Household Cavalry's musical rides and quadrilles? Short of the Changing of the Guard and Trooping the Colour, has this country any better traditional displays to offer? Men and horses are hand-picked. Fewer than 30 out of 250 receive the honour of finding a place in their fraternities, perhaps 14 from The Life Guards and 14 from the Blues and Royals, the best, in every way, of soldier and horse. Sefton was one of the elite, not of the trick rides – his white markings debarred him from those – but of the equestrian ballet, in which he performed at Olympia, Wembley and Windsor, at the Royal Welsh Show and the Essex County Show, at Basingstoke, Chichester, Malvern, Glamorgan, Wimbledon and Ardingly. On occasions he was obliged to live rough. From marquees to auction rooms, from market places to cowsheds, he has had a taste of every sort of makeshift stabling.

Round and round he and his co-stars went, lance pennants a-flutter, now like a part of the spokes of a spiralling wheel, now in tight circles, now cantering, now trotting, now in a vortex, now in a crossing of paths; Life Guards in scarlet and white, Blues and Royals in blue and crimson, making a buoyant rhythm to the tunes of *Lillibulero* and *Light Cavalry, Guildhall* and

Boots and Saddles, the trumpet march of *Fehrbelliner Reitersmarsch*, the canter of *Brandenburger*, the lance drill of *Schreewaltzer* and the regimental marches, *Aida* and *Keel Row*. Obedient, good on acceleration, quick on the turn and with a swaggering presence to match, Sefton was just the type the Riding Master wanted.

By 1979, however, when he was sixteen, his worn foreleg tendons rendered him susceptible to lameness. He was deemed too great a physical liability to take any further part. It seemed that he had had his day in the sun.

By the time of the Royal Wedding he was 18, an age which, on average, probably marks the culmination of a Household Cavalry horse's active life. In 1981 he might have passed into obscurity, forgotten by all except a handful of Blues and Royals who had enjoyed some sport or competition successes or ceremonial duties on his generous, willing back. But, in 1982, fate brought him back into the limelight.

By April of that year – shortly after the State Visit of the Sultan of Oman – there was drama in the air for the Blues and Royals. On the 6th morning of the month two medium reconnaissance troops, of the service regiment then stationed at Windsor, equipped with Scimitar and Scorpion armoured cars, set sail from Plymouth in SS Canberra. By the third week of May they had landed in the Falkland Islands. By mid-June, in close support of the 3rd Battalion of the Parachute Regiment and the 1st Battalions of the Scots and Welsh Guards, they had fought their way from Bluff Cove and Fitzroy to Mount Tumbledown. Their efficient and gallant participation in the campaign was not much reported. The following month, however, their comrades in the Mounted Squadron made front-page headlines. The name of one of the horses was echoed across the world. It was Sefton.

Quadrille. Sefton's white markings debarred him from this part of the Household Cavalry Musical Ride. (Mike Roberts)

11 The Fateful Morning

06.00 hours. Tuesday July 20, 1982. The Household Cavalry Mounted Regiment was awakened by the trumpeter's *reveille*. For 450 men and 250 horses another busy day was about to begin. In the stalls of Number Three Troop, of the Blues and Royals Squadron, stood an old black horse with a white blaze and four white socks, a widely experienced veteran with a mind of his own. The melodramatic and agonising circumstances of this day were about to make his name resound through Britain and Ireland, and right round the world.

Sefton's first activity that morning was half-an-hour's exercise in the riding school. All the horses that are earmarked for Queen's Life Guard start the day with a 'blanket ride'. Their ceremonial walk to Whitehall only takes 30 minutes, and otherwise that is the only exercise they would have.

06.20 hours. The heavy, electrically-controlled double doors of the riding school swung open for the first time in the morning, and those who, a little over four hours later, would be riding to the Horse Guards, Whitehall, resplendent in cuirass and helmet, now filed across the school's tan floor in denims, inelegant crash helmets and ankle boots, while their black horses – and one grey (the trumpeter's) – wore a single blanket, strapped on by a surcingle.

'*Ride ter-rot!*' shouted the Corporal-of-Horse, and the great high-ceilinged riding school reverberated to padded hoofbeats, occasional equine snorts and the knock of feet against the wooden walls. *Leading file, change the rein!... Ride, at the quarter marker ... right incline...!*

The 'sit-down trot', uncomfortable for most horsemen, is stock-in-trade for the Household Cavalryman. Sefton, with his bold presence, stood out among the others, and Trooper Michael Pedersen, an easy horseman, a Cornishman of London origin, tall and military moustachioed, looked just right on him. Sefton's age was 19, Pedersen's 21.

The voice of the Corporal-of-Horse echoed across the school again: *Ride can-ter!* Sefton responded with fluent rhythm to the pressure of Pedersen's legs. Sefton was not Pedersen's regular ride. The man whose name had been coupled with the horse up to July 20 was Trooper Adrian Philips. Few members of the Blues and Royals Mounted Squadron could remember an occasion when Philips and Sefton were not awarded a 'box' at Horse Guards, that is to say had not been among the four members of the Queen's Life Guard singled out by the Adjutant as the best trooper-and-horse combinations on parade, with the honour of mounting guard in front of the Whitehall sentry-boxes – at the 'Gateway to London', as it is traditionally

Work had already begun in the fire-blazing forge. (Leslie Lane)

called – as distinct from the dismounted sentries, whose more humble beat is in the Horse Guards forecourt.

In 1980 Lance-Corporal John Dickens won the Princess Elizabeth Cup with Sefton. First presented by Her Majesty two years before she came to the throne, this prize is awarded annually to the best turned-out combination of horse-and-soldier in the Household Cavalry Regiment, the final being between those who have secured the most 'boxes' during the previous year. That made Sefton, in 1980, the pre-eminent horse in the barracks.

Just eight weeks before this morning of July the 20th, Pedersen had won the coveted trophy with a horse called Higgins.

Why was Sefton not carrying his accustomed rider today? By coincidence Philips was on leave. Otherwise he, not Pedersen, would have been astride Sefton. Cavalrymen like Philips grow to respect and love their horses; they become jealous about them to the point of possessiveness. If Philips had been there, no other soldier would have taken Sefton on Guard.

06.45 hours. *Ride ter-rot... Ride wa-a-lk!... Leading file, left turn...* The Corporal-of-Horse pressed the button that opened the double doors, the soldiers led their horses across the parade ground and up the concrete incline leading to the Blues and Royals quarters. 'Reveille Stables' were nearly over. The pungent smell of ammonia on straw rose from the column of bedding now piled between the rows of stalls as the other dutymen finished mucking out.

Feed away! Sefton settled his nose into his manger – the grind of his teeth on oats, bran and chaff was part of a munching chorus – while Pedersen and his mates strode away to the cookhouse. July 20 did not look like bringing anything out of the ordinary to either horse or rider. Routine days never do.

08.00 hours. There was bustle in the Barracks. The exercise party for the horses that were not down for any particular duty, known as the 'watering order', had just returned from its hour's trot around the London streets; regimental policemen and clerks, storemen and farriers, cooks and orderlies crossed the parade-ground about their business, and work had already begun in the fire-blazing forge. A recruits' ride was filing into the school for its first instruction of the day. Rough-riding instructors, smart as whips in blue patrol tunics and scarlet-striped breeches, urged their nervous remounts over the motor-hectic road to put them through their paces in the Park, where one or two officers were already exercising their chargers – and their dogs, too.

Those whose destiny it was to be on Queen's Life Guard led their horses from the troop stalls and tied them to the wall-rings, in the passage between the tack rooms and the stables, to start the most energetic part of their routine: grooming.

If Pedersen was to be awarded a 'box', Sefton's black body must shine as bright as quartz. For the next hour the trooper's body brush swept over that coat with unpausing concentration, the brush was scraped on the curry comb, and time and again the curry comb was knocked clean of dirt. Sefton's nostrils were sponged, his mane and tail were brushed with the care of a starlet's hair, his blaze and his four white socks were chalk-powdered to strike the eye like the dazzle of new-fallen snow, and his feet were oiled, so that his squadron number, RHG/D 61 and his army number, 5816, which were inscribed there 14 years before, glistened beautifully. Sefton was not an easy horse to groom. He had a reputation in Three Troop for regarding the process as something of a comedy. From time to time he swung his old head round and gave Pedersen a jocular nip. Some say that, on those occasions, he seemed still to be smiling when he faced the front again.

Pedersen lifted the heavy cavalry saddle – its black sheepskin cover rising in a roll over the shoe-cases and cape, strapped on the front arch – onto Sefton's back, and, as he went to tighten the blanco-white girth, the old gelding gave a quick wriggle and a sidestep (whether from playfulness or sheer ticklishness, Sefton always does that. It would be in character if it was leg-pulling).

Next came the bridle, with the S-shaped curb-piece carrying on each side its crests, lions flanked by the words 'Peninsular' above and 'Waterloo' below, emphasising the triumphs whereby the Blues were raised, in 1820, to the status of Household Cavalry, alongside their time-honoured comrades-in-arms, The Life Guards. Sefton wore his saddlery with apparent pride. Indeed he seemed to be made for a 'box'. But would his trooper come up to scratch? No one, who was familiar with Pedersen's performance, thought otherwise.

09.00 hours. Leaving his horse tethered to the wall-ring Pedersen crossed over to the Knightsbridge side of the barracks and climbed the stairs leading to the room he shared with two other men from his troop, a room redolent of brasso and pin-ups, boot polish, uniforms and football stars. He put on his white buckskin breeches, then his stiff-leather jackboots, winged at the thigh – carrying so many coats of black polish that their veneer gave the impression of deeply-lustred lacquer – and completed by a pair of white-metal, swan-necked spurs. He strapped his sword belt around his waist, buttoned his tunic, and, with the help of his mate, concealed most of it with his cuirasses (the glistening breastplate and backplate, relics of the medieval knight-in-armour and not worn on active service since the 17th century). Then, when he had slipped the white blancoed cartouche belt under his shoulder strap for his friend to fasten at the back, he took the red horsehair plume from its holder and screwed it into his helmet, ensuring that not a hair was out of place.

09.30. He put on his helmet, picked up his gauntlets and sword, and inspected himself in the mirror. Yes, he thought, now I look every inch a worthy match for Sefton.

From those high windows of the Blues and Royals troop rooms, the soldiers can peer west past Prince's Gate, in the direction of Albert Hall, and east along Knightsbridge towards Hyde Park Corner. Not more than 400 yards east from where Pedersen stood, evil men, men who hate Britain, who hate, above all, the British Army, lay in deadly ambush. Such peril was the last thing on Pedersen's mind. The nearest sensation he felt to fear that morning was, perhaps, a fleeting sensation that through some unlucky mishap, he and Sefton might not be awarded a 'box'.

10.00 hours. Cavalry horses, like soldiers, are gregarious creatures, they merge into line as elegantly as swallows alighting, wing to wing, on telegraph wires. So the Queen's Life Guard lined up on the parade ground of Hyde Park Barracks ... and numbered off, *1 – 2, 1 – 2!* The odd numbers marched forward so that there was plenty of space for the inspection party. Captain Scott, the Adjutant – assisted by Mr Lawson, the Regimental Corporal Major – now began his close scrutiny, finding the minutest imperfections, a curb chain too tight, a dull noseband, a tarnished buckle, a slightly crooked helmet, a blemished gauntlet, a spur with a fleck of rust, a stirrup boss with a boot-polish stain, a mane not quite brushed down, the suggestion of dust on a sheepskin, a hoof not properly oiled, a white browband bearing a speck of dirt, faults probably imperceptible to the lay eye. Points, awarded or deducted, were duly recorded by the orderly corporal.

10.25 hours. *Slope swords! Sit at ease! Shun! Car-ry swords! Rear rank, wa-alk march!... Guard, rein back!* Sefton, wise old horse, had done as many guards as any other on parade. He stood as though to attention, rock still, his nose pulled in, giving him a bent-at-the-poll look, like a warrior horse of old. When those with the highest number of points awarded on the inspection, the four 'boxmen', were called forward, predictably Pedersen, with Sefton, was among them.

The Captain of the Guard, Lieutenant Daly, making his debut in that role, now rode on parade. (Might a veteran observer have been present, one who would have noted that when Lieutenant Daly's father and grandfather – both of whom served in the Royal Horse Guards (the Blues) – mounted Guard, their chargers lacked the black plume that hangs from the bridle of a Blues and Royals' officer's charger? The innovation came when the 1st Royal Dragoons, whose accoutrement it was, were amalgamated with the Blues.)

Lieutenant Daly reined his charger, Falcon, to the front of the Guard. *Take or-der... March!* he shouted. *Escort to receive the Standard, walk ... march!* A regimental policeman lifted the Royal Standard onto the socket on Corporal-Major Ronald Bright's boot. Bright and his escort rode back to their places. *Carry swords!* Lieutenant Daly's trumpeter sounded the Royal salute. *Close or-der, march! Half-sections, left, walk march!*

10.35 hours. To the music of a second Royal salute, the Queen's Life Guard, 16 men and 16 horses, passed under the arch of the barrack gate – with its huge stone pediment of prancing steeds that once adorned the riding-school of the old Knightsbridge barracks. They turned right, down the middle of the road, between the lanes of roaring traffic. Two mounted policemen joined the procession, one in front, one behind. Their horses were called Echo and Eclipse. It was a peaceful, sunny, day: cotton-wool clouds broke up the blue, joggers warmed up on the pavements, Hyde Park's plane trees were dressed for high summer, horsemen and women enjoyed Rotton Row, gulls gyrated over the Serpentine where people with brown paper bags were feeding the ducks; and both visitors to Britain and Londoners, who were walking their dogs, pushing prams, strolling to their offices or simply stretching their legs, stopped for a moment to look at this familiar yet freshly resplendent, breath-taking sight – Her Majesty's Life Guard riding down the South Carriageway to take over their duties at Whitehall. The soldiers looked very hot in their

'The great beasts lay on their sides, looking pitiful,' said an eye-witness press reporter, 'their eyes half-starting out of their sockets.' (Press Association)

'Many who witnessed the scene, who saw those black bodies, once vibrant and powerful, once glowing with good health, will never erase the pathos from their memories.' (London Express Service; Press Association)

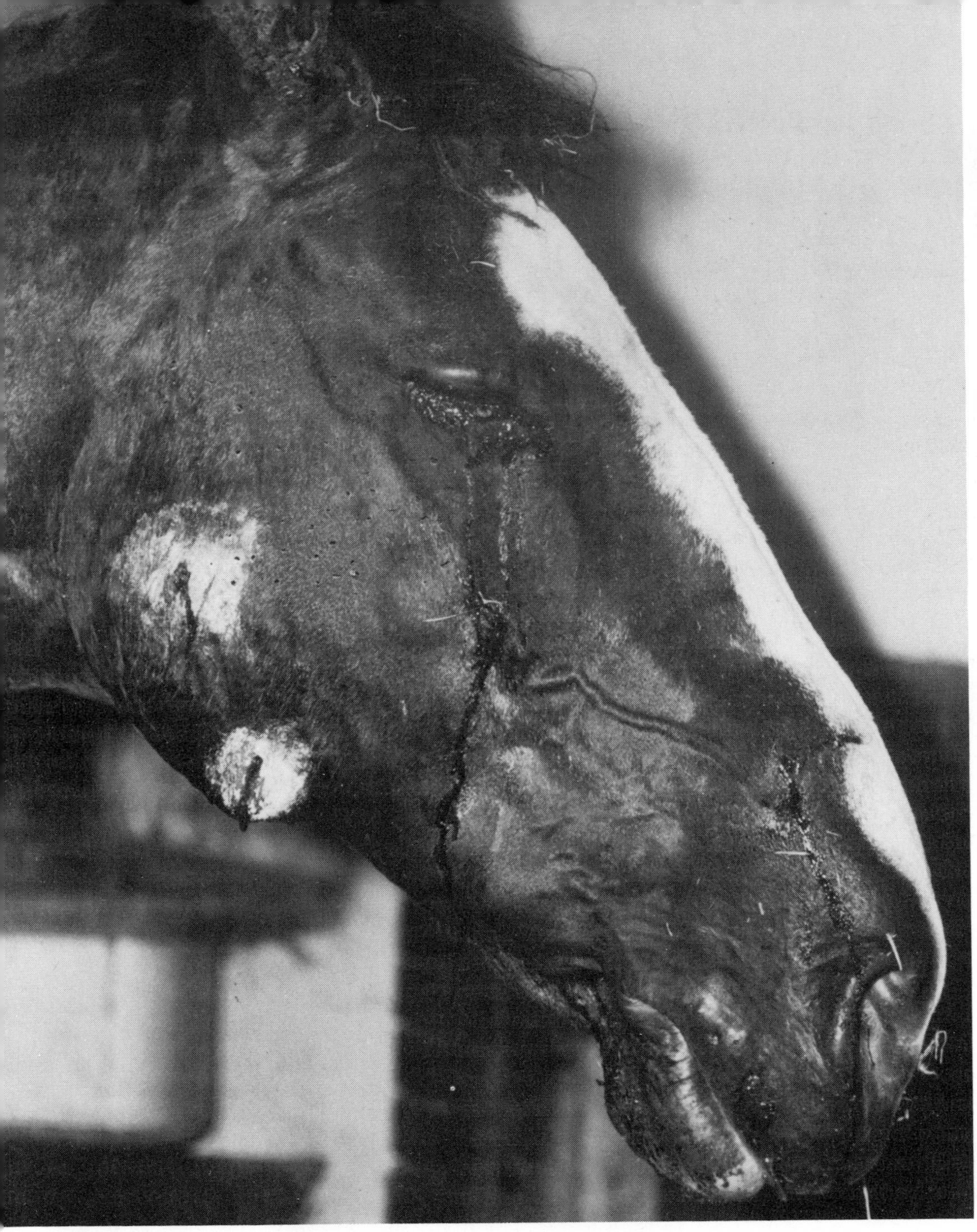

(Left): *‘Sefton, weak and shattered, one eye closed up, so that he could hardly see on the offside, was led slowly back towards the barracks. (London Express Service)*

(Above): *One of the four-inch nails removed from Sefton's body after the bombing. (Press Association)*

thick serge tunics and cuirasses.

In less than half-an-hour's time this Guard – in which Sefton had his place on the right-hand side, a half-section from the rear – would line up opposite The Life Guards at Whitehall, to fulfil the Blues and Royals/Life Guards alternation, which has been traditional since the Second World War.* Or would they?

* Before the War, when the two regiments of Household Cavalry, The Life Guards and the Blues, were entirely horsed, they alternated annually between London and Windsor.

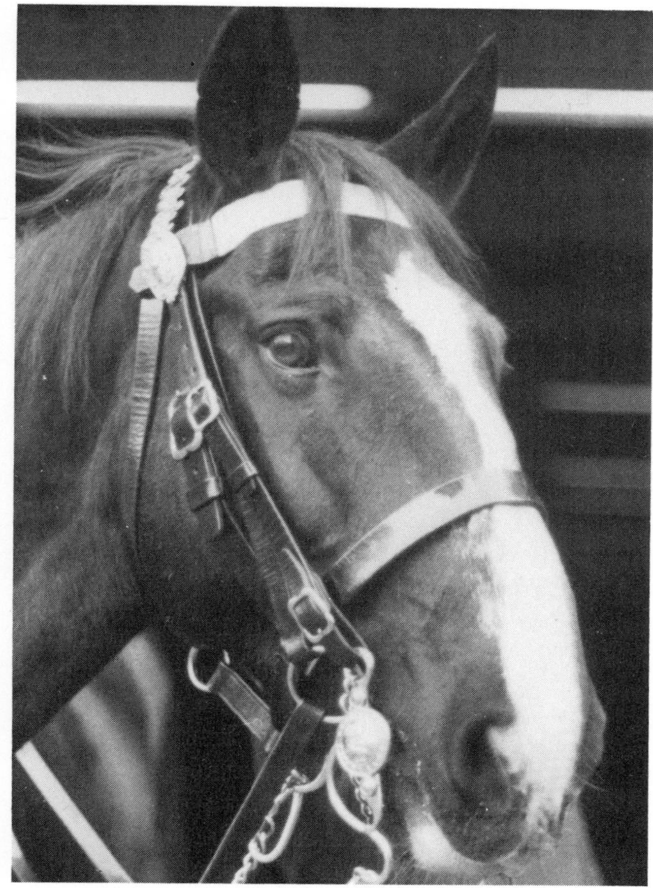

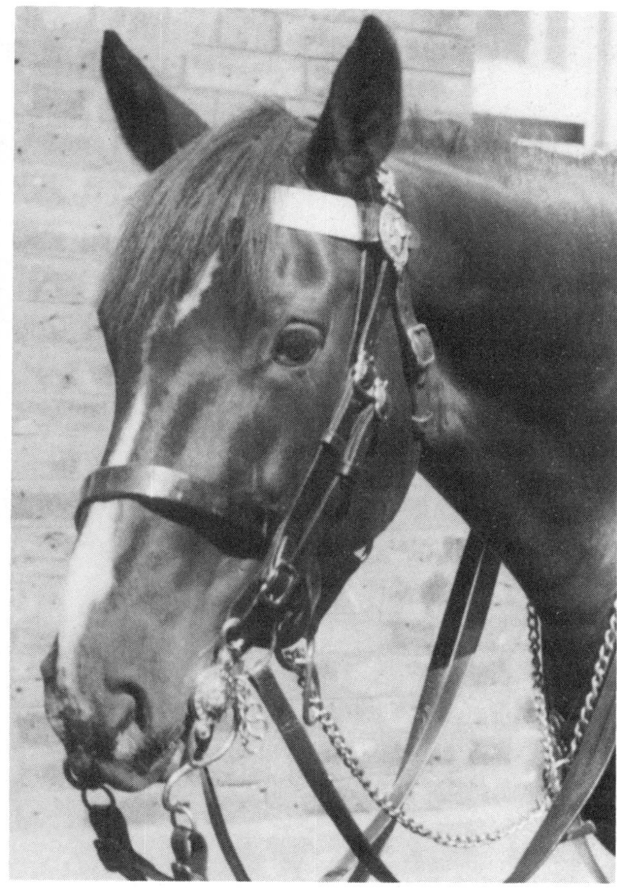

Two of Sefton's stable-mates who were victims of the attack: Waterford (left) *and* Eclipse (right). *Waterford was killed under the late Corporal-Major Ronald Bright who carried the standard, and Eclipse was badly injured.*

In less than half-an-hour Lieutenant Daly's mother, now waiting at the Horse Guards, would watch proudly as her son went through his paces for the first time. Or would she? In half-an-hour's time Sefton would be standing as he had so often stood before, in front of one of those coveted sentry-boxes. Or would he?

The public are inclined to forget that the Household Cavalry have rendered themselves the enemies of the Queen's enemies at least as much as any other branch of Her Majesty's armed forces. They overlook the fact that the tank and armoured car are more habitually their vehicles than the equine mount; that the operational elements of this world-famous Corps are nearly three times as large as the ceremonial; that the Household Cavalryman is trained, too, as a tank and armoured car driver and gunner, as a radio operator, rifleman and machine-gunner, with all the attendant technical expertise that those trades imply and modern warfare demands. Perhaps it is not generally appreciated that these cavaliers of the Queen play their part, on foreign and active service, on equal terms with all the other corps and regiments.

It was not easy for the man-in-the-street to identify the crewmen of the two Blues and Royals troops of Scorpion and Scimitar armoured cars, who had –

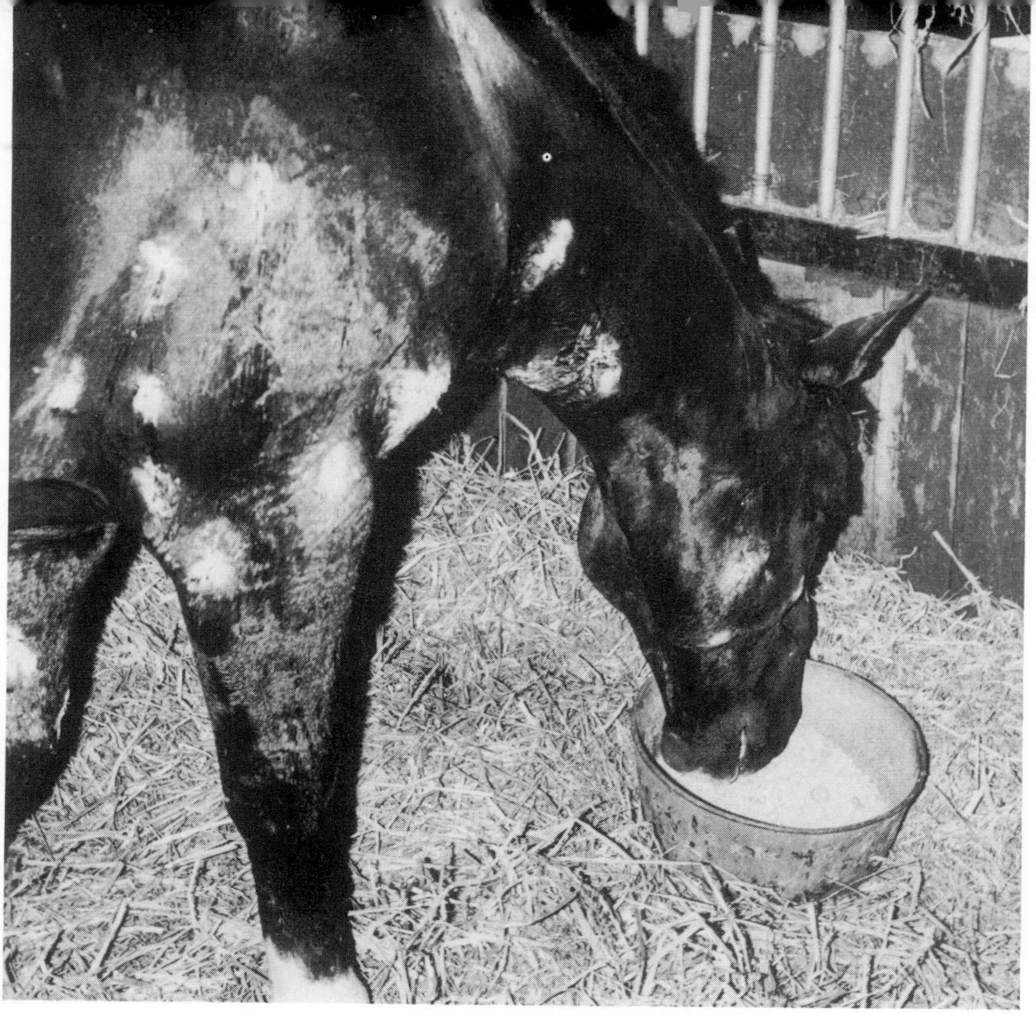

'He was eating a bran mash by the evening.' (Mike Roberts)

after several days' brave and skilful fighting, recently entered Port Stanley, with the 2nd Battalion of the Parachute Regiment – with those dazzling figures now riding to Whitehall. Not once, but time and again, over the past decade, the Blues and Royals have made enemies in Ulster, too. The mauve-and-green General Service Medal, with its clasp labelled 'Northern Ireland', now glinting on the chests of Lieutenant Daly, Corporal-Major Bright and Corporal-of-Horse Pitt, was testimony to that.

Ireland? The Household Cavalry Mounted Regiment has an association of a different kind with the Emerald Isle. That vivid-grass country and the genus *equus* are practically synonymous. Nearly all the Household Cavalry horses come from there. Every horse on Guard that day – with the exception of one – was foaled and bought by the Army from Southern Ireland.

10.38 hours. How many times in his ceremonial life has Sefton walked past the Hyde Park Hotel? 300? 400? He passed it now. But July 20 would not see him to Hyde Park Corner.

10.40 – 10.41 hours. During this minute the IRA committed the crime that was probably to bring them more enemies than any other in their iniquitous and cowardly career. They had placed in a parked car a bomb composed of some 25lb of gelignite-based explosive, surrounded by 30lb of 6-inch and 4-inch nails, and, as the centre of the Queen's Life Guard drew level, they

Corporal-Major (SQMC) Bright, the Standard Bearer on the Fateful Morning, photographed when he was a member of the team that won the Household Division tug-of-war championship.

detonated it by radio control. Let an eye-witness take up the narrative:

> The moment that will haunt me for the rest of my days arrived at 10.40 and 23 seconds yesterday morning. I am so precise because my first, unthinking, reflex was to look at my watch. And then the full horror of the carnage in Hyde Park enveloped and engulfed me, and almost blotted out my consciousness. Seconds before, the world had been a different place. Now it was irrevocably changed, and nothing would ever seem the same again. Seconds before it had been a beautiful summer day, and I had been driving to work down the South Carriage Road towards Knightsbridge. Then the traffic lights changed to red, and I slowed to a halt. Idly, I watched a detachment of Household Cavalry clip-clopping down the road 100 yards ahead of me, plumes dancing, breast and backplates gleaming in the sun, their horses groomed and their equipment burnished.
>
> It was at that moment that my bright red Ford Cortina car shook as the very earth trembled under me. It was at that moment that I looked at my watch. A ball of flame shooting into the air was the first sign that a catastrophe had happened. This was immediately followed by an ear-splitting thud and a column of black smoke. But it was what I witnessed a few moments later that will live with me forever. Suddenly robbed of all humanity, they (the soldiers) became grotesque figures, dazed and wandering among the stricken animals or lying dreadfully still. And there was the terrible, total, complete silence – a silence so absolute that it chilled the mind and the senses. A complete vacuum of noise. Not one

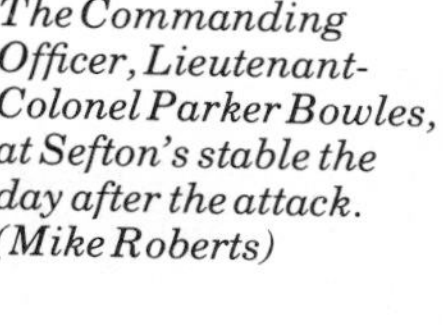

The Commanding Officer, Lieutenant-Colonel Parker Bowles, at Sefton's stable the day after the attack. (Mike Roberts)

The tattered Standard of the Blues and Royals Squadron. It was carried aloft by the Corporal-Major of the next Blues and Royals Queen's Life Guard two days later. (Mike Roberts)

horse made a single sound. No whinnying. No snorting. The great beasts lay on their sides or half sitting-up, looking pitiful, their eyes half starting out of their sockets. One or two of the stronger or less seriously wounded horses were somehow remaining on their haunches, looking around with almost human panic and shock in their huge brown eyes. Now I saw more red. The bright, glistening red of the blood that started to seep, and sometimes spurt, from the glossy black coats of the horses. They had been scythed to ribbons by the thousands of nails and bolts packed around the infernal device planted in that hum-drum looking car. At last, when I was beginning to wonder if that dreadful scene was to be frozen for all time, some of the less seriously injured troopers staggered to their feet. I watched, mesmerised, at what happened next. For every single man who could walk reacted in the same way.

They started to look around for their horses ... to see they were all right ... to catch the ones that had struggled to their feet. Instinctively, the troopers cared more for their horses than themselves. Of course, each man was concerned for his comrades – but, first, they wanted to look after their terribly muted horses. By now, the horses were clearly in more pain. They were still making no noise, but they had that look in their eyes ... Nearly everything on which I place my values had been shattered with this terrible, cowardly act of violence. And my first angry thought was that it had been so easy for the terrorists. The car in which the bomb had been placed was, by now, burning from end to end. And there was a stench of burning flesh and blood in the air. It may seem as if

Trooper Pedersen's jackboot, showing the bomb damage. (Leslie Lane)

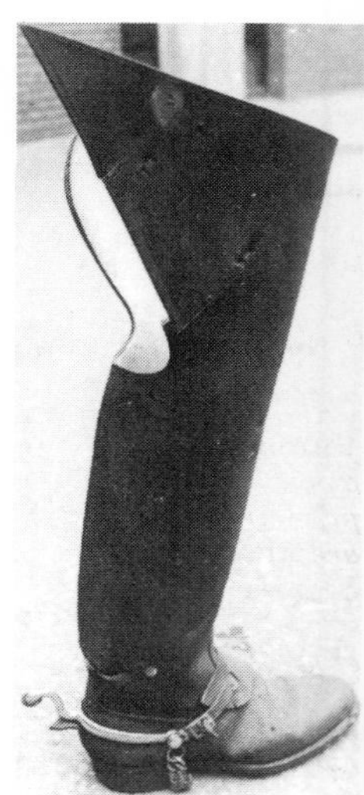

> I was only concentrating on the horses. Well, really, I was. The troopers are so small in comparison, and it was hard to spot them as they lay among their beautiful steeds, hidden by the thrashing legs and the sheer bulk of the horses. But then two young troopers, who had run from Knightsbridge Barracks after hearing the explosion, started to lead horses away from the scene. I asked one of them whether he had seen what had happened. He was crying, too, and all he could do was shake his head. The surviving horses, pouring blood from jagged flesh wounds, looked oddly peaceful as they were led back to the stables.*

Lieutenant Daly, Corporal-Major Bright, Lance-Corporal Young and Trooper Tipper were dead or dying. Yeastvite, Epaulette, Rochester, Waterford, Falcon, Zara and Cedric, either kneeling or lying, eyes dilated with panic and shock and pain, were never to raise themselves to their feet again. The Regimental Corporal-Major, Mr Lawson, was quick enough onto the scene to see a policeman's pistol at their heads, to witness them put out of their agony. The police horses, Eclipse and Echo, were badly hurt.

And Sefton? He and Eclipse (of the Blues and Royals) and Copenhagen were the injured ones, Eclipse badly, Copenhagen and Sefton close to death.

'I was dazed, I did not know what the hell had happened,' relates Pedersen. 'Sefton just stood there, head hanging, feet splayed, gushing blood. I heard voices, through the smoke, telling me to "get off your horse!"'

Nails had penetrated Sefton all over his off side, the most serious going

* James Whitaker, *Daily Star*, 21.7.82.

Victims of the attack at a press interview the following day. They are the Trumpeter, Stephen Sullivan, and (right) *Corporal-of-Horse James Pitt. Lieutenant-Colonel Parker Bowles stands behind. (Press Association)*

deep into a point above his stifle. A six-inch nail was driven through his bridle into his head. Fireballs had scorched his eyeball, there were chips of car metal across his neck. Worst of all, a razor-sharp chunk of car metal had severed his jugular vein. Those four white socks that were chalk-powdered to snowy perfection a minute ago were now blood-stained almost beyond recognition. The old gelding was losing blood fast.

The Regiment's Commanding Officer, Lieutenant-Colonel A.H. Parker Bowles*, a decorated veteran of the Rhodesian Peacekeeping Force of 1980, and another who wears the 'Northern Ireland' clasp on his General Service Medal, was standing on the balcony outside the orderly room. 'The last time I heard anything like that ominous explosion, he said afterwards, 'was in Londonderry in 1972...'

> ...At 10.45 on July 20 soldiers were running back and forth, helter-skelter, below me. Everyone's instinct was 'Oh, my God, the Guard!' Then I heard one of the farriers say, 'The bastards have got the horses!' and I ran through the gate and down the South Carriageway as fast as I could. The first thing that caught my eye, through the smoke, was a tree in flames. I saw Pedersen standing, half-conscious, with a nail pierced through the gauntlet of his right hand and through his little finger, but still holding Sefton, from whose jugular the blood was visibly pumping. A Life Guard Corporal-of-Horse, O'Flaherty, who had doubled up to the scene, had his fist on the wound, feeling for the pressure point. He was covered in blood. I told him to get a shirt, or something, and stuff it into the hole, which he did...

Sefton, weak and shattered, one eye closed up so that he could hardly see on his off side, was led slowly back towards the barracks. Halfway down the road a regimental horsebox was waiting for him. He ambled up the ramp, was held steady in the vehicle and was soon in the sanctuary of veterinary care. Veterinary-Major Carding, who had been tending the other horses at the scene of the explosion, cobbled up the glaring neck wound and that point above the stifle and two other places. He applied ligatures and antibiotics and fly repellent. He gave Sefton a fifty-fifty hope of recovery.

The Green Jackets band, playing in Regent's Park that morning, were also bombed into hideous death and injury. Yet, of the two crimes, without hesitation the nation deemed the one against the Household Cavalry to be the worse. Many who witnessed the scene, who saw those black bodies, once vibrant and powerful, a moment before in perfect health, but now prostrate, feeble, vainly kicking the air or raising their heads with a pleading look in their eyes – even people who gained only a distant view of it on their television screens that evening – will never erase the pathos from their memories. Was that because animals are so devoid of malice, so impeccably innocent, so undeserving of involvement in the quarrels of man, yet so vulnerable to his cruelty and hatred? Perhaps it was because the noble horse, of all the domestic creatures, is so unstinting in his duty, so full of fortitude,

Trumpeter Sullivan and Gauntlet. Riding in advance of the Guard they received only minor injuries. (Press Association)

* Well known on the Turf, Colonel Parker Bowles rode in the 1969 Grand National, and, with Pakie, won the Grand Military Gold Cup in 1974.

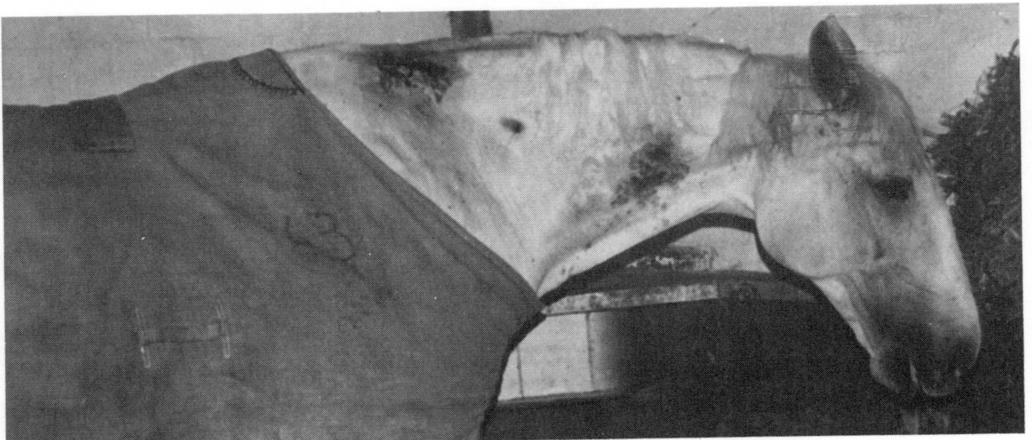

The police horse Eclipse photographed the day after the bombing. (Mike Roberts)

so silent in his agony, that when he suffers it makes man ashamed for the human race?

When, on July 22, the next Blues and Royals Guard rode down to relieve The Life Guards at Whitehall, they carried aloft the Royal Squadron Standard which had been tattered to shreds two days before; and Londoners, for whom Sefton was already a name that brought waves of affection to the heart and tears to the eyes, cheered them to the echo.

A horse remembers. If, indeed, he did not possess a very retentive memory, it would not be possible for man to train him, step by step, in all the sophisticated movements and disciplines that Sefton, for example, had been taught 14 years before. And although he does not have the power of thought and reflection, as we know it, surely he experiences instinctive images of his past? A human being's memories, arising from the subconscious, are said to be often strongest when he is in a coma or on drugs, or coming through some severe physical crisis.

If such a principle is applicable to a horse, and if ever Sefton received strong mental images of his past, would they not have been particularly vivid after the horror of July the 20th? Possibly his whole life from colthood in County Waterford to rejection at Wellington Barracks, from stardom in Germany to glory on Royal Wedding day, streamed across his consciousness, as a motion picture flickers on a screen. He stood in the valley of the shadow of death. Most horses, as badly injured as he was, would have succumbed. Not resilient Sefton; he was eating a bran mash by the evening. Did he know that an act of man, not of God, had mutilated him? Whether or not he knew, in his fine heart there was no trace of hatred for man.

Soon Police notices appeared in public places all over London. They were read with more interest than usual. 'MURDER' announced the placard, depicting a bearded man. 'About 30. 5 feet 8 inches tall, proportionate build. Brown hair. Irish accent. Bombs exploded in Regent's Park and Hyde Park, July 20. Suspected of these offences.' Apart from relations and friends of the men who were killed and wounded, animal lovers, in particular, would not forgive – not in a thousand years.

12 The Horse of the Year

Every head across the bar
Every blaze and snip and star
Every nervous twitching ear
Every soft eye filled with fear
Seeks a friend and seems to say
Whither now and where away?
Seeks a friend and seems to ask
Where the goal and what the task . . . ?

There goes timid childlike trust
To the burden and the dust!
High-born courage, princely grace
To the peril it must face!
There go stoutness, strength and speed
To be spent where none shall heed
And great hearts to face their fate
In the clash of human hate!*

Those verses by Will Ogilvie speak of freshly-trained remounts arriving in Flanders to take their place in the order of battle, oblivious of the horrors that awaited them in the front line; ready, in their innocence, to put every ounce of their energy and their will into whatever was asked of them. There were officers and men at Hyde Park Barracks whose grandfathers and great-grandfathers, having served in the Great War with The Life Guards, the Royal Horse Guards or the 1st Royal Dragoons, might have told them of the horrors and the carnage, of chargers and troop-horses cut to ribbons by shell and bomb, or by wire and machine gun, lying, perhaps with broken legs, for hours before they lost consciousness or a kind bullet relieved them of their torment. The havoc of July the 20th, a small reminder of the sort of misery that cavalry horses endured 60 years and more ago, prompted philosophical horse-lovers everywhere to thank God that, for the most part, mankind no longer subjects its animals to the battlefield, to what Ogilvie called 'the clash of human hate'.

The pharmacy yard at Hyde Park Barracks, looking like a cavalry surgical centre in the wars of yore, was still awash with blood when, at lunchtime, the second IRA attack occurred (cutting through the Green Jackets band, as they

* From *The Remount Train* by Will H. Ogilvie

Household Cavalrymen and their horses in the film The Last Cavalry Charge. *'The havoc of July 20 prompted philosophical horse-lovers everywhere to thank God that mankind no longer subjects its animals to the battlefield.'*

'Prince Philip called at the Barracks again in the morning.'

Farrier-Major (FQMC) Smith and Zany. 'Mountains of fruit and vegetables for the horses.' (Press Association)

Two weeks after the bombing, PC John Davis takes his horse Echo for their first walk together in Hyde Park. Both were injured by the blast. (Press Association)

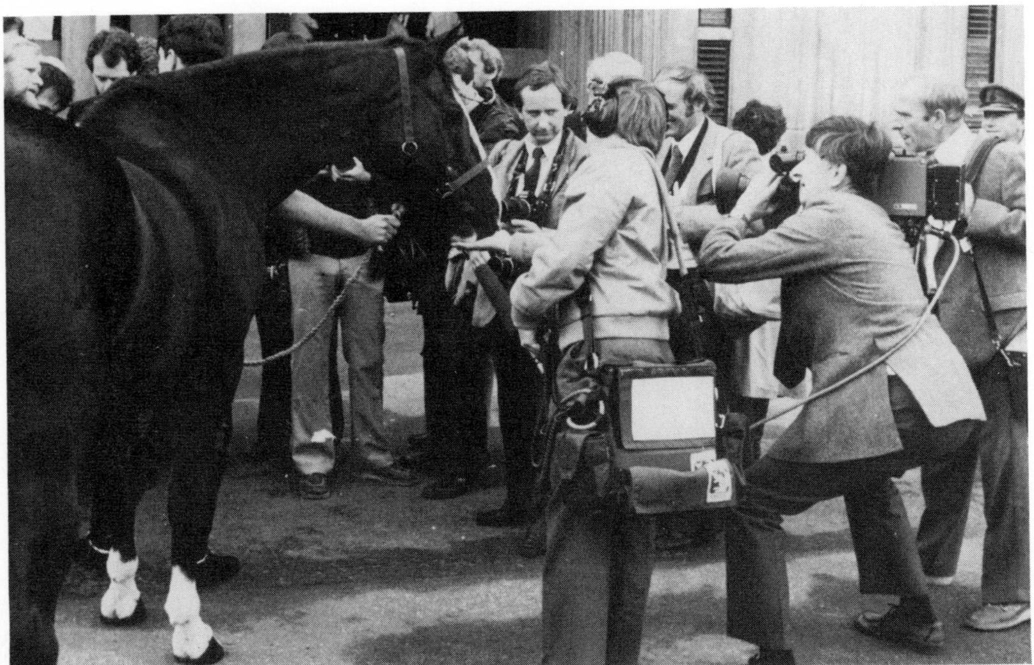

Sefton and the Press. 'The people of Britain wanted a name upon which to focus their compassion and their admiration.' (Mike Roberts)

played in Regent's Park, to murder another seven innocents). It was not until 3.0 o'clock the following morning that Veterinary-Major Carding and Farrier-Major (FQMC) Smith completed their basic work of tending the wounded horses. Of the eight injured survivors, Copenhagen came closest to death, but Sefton's severed jugular was the most serious of the lesions.

There was no longer a 'front line' in Britain's emergencies and wars; or, if there was, the streets of London belonged to it as well as the streets of Belfast. A devastating, cowardly blow had been struck at her Majesty's Life Guard; the man who had commanded it was dead and the one who had carried her Standard lay dying in hospital. And how passionately the Queen felt that it was a blow at her!

Since April she had been on tenterhooks over Prince Andrew's mission in the Falklands. Just recently she had suffered the shocks of the Palace intruder and the Trestrail affair, and she had been admitted to hospital for the first time in her life. The previous weekend one of her closest friends and confidants* had died. Now came this – this bloody, cowardly, unprecedented assault on her Life Guard. It was almost too much to bear. Yet, only a few hours later, she was required to smile politely at a Garden Party. That evening she telephoned Colonel Parker Bowles and spoke to him from the heart for ten minutes. As a devotee of the horse, by now she knew the names of Sefton and the others, and she pitied them as passionately and genuinely as anyone in Britain. Prince Philip called at the barracks to see the survivors in the morning, and Princess Anne arrived in the evening.

Within 24 hours Colonel Parker Bowles had received messages from every

* Lord Rupert Nevill

member of the Royal Family, not to mention the Pope and the Prime Minister. The response from the nation – and from many other parts of the world, too – was overwhelming. For the next two weeks the barracks was deluged with presents, among them six crates of whisky from Harrods for the injured men. The stallholders of Covent Garden sent mountains of fruit and vegetables for the horses, and, to quote only one other item, a quarter of a million *Polo* mints were received.

The Commanding Officer was obliged to set aside a large room to hold all the gifts, two clerks were appointed to run it and two officers to receive the press and the presents and to thank the benefactors. Donations amounting to some £100,000 poured in, among the largest of the cheques being those from the National Farmers' Union and from members of the Knightsbridge Association. Get-well cards arrived thick as confetti. They were pinned all over the door and walls of Sefton's box. 'Cheat the bastards,' one of them exhorted him, 'live!'

The people of Britain wanted a name upon which to focus their compassion and their admiration. And it was Sefton, with his vivid and engaging

Sefton and Veterinary-Major Carding. (London Express Service)

character, his outstanding forebearance, his particular facility for touching the heart, who supplied that focus. His name and his picture were splashed across the popular press. Daily bulletins on the state of his recovery were eagerly and apprehensively awaited in every part of Britain and Ireland – 'this Irish horse, wantonly tortured by Irishmen.'

Early in August, while the Regiment prepared for camp, the eight horses that had been injured – Quo Minus, Eclipse, Zany, Ringlet, Bandit, Salamander, Copenhagen and Sefton – were boxed up to the Royal Army Veterinary Corps Depot at Melton Mowbray, a place that Sefton may have remembered from his early remount days in 1967. There their wounds were washed and dressed again, and the more serious cases were X-rayed to ensure that no pieces of metal remained under their skin. Everyone at Melton was amazed at Sefton's resilience, at how quickly he was recovering, and what a good 'doer' he was (a reminder of Corporal Batey's verdict in Germany: 'He'd have looked good on sawdust, that one!')

Corporal Islay Forbes, of the Women's Royal Army Corps, a girl who had nursed and loved many horses, commented to me on Sefton's 'great common sense... He knew exactly what was wanted of him in the stable and out. He took everything in his stride here... Ooh, he was cheeky though! You should have seen the nips he took at me. All in fun, of course!'

At Melton many people addressed poems to him; some offered to live in his loose-box and be his lifelong nurse; some applied, earnestly, for nails and other pieces of metal from his body; others harboured quaint ideas of mercy: 'It would be a crying shame for anyone to get on his back again. Don't imprison him in a stable! Let him roam free!'

Several months went by before the groundswell of public emotion subsided. Terence Cuneo painted a portrait of Sefton, entitled *Outrage*, hanging his head and showing all his traumas. Far from the splendour of his image of panoply, he was held by a denim-clad farrier. The picture was sold at auction for over £12,000 in aid of the Army Benevolent Fund. 15,000 greetings cards were printed from it in the same cause and, amazingly for so unfestive a subject, all of them were bought within three weeks.

Sefton ashtrays, Sefton medallions and Sefton pendants were purchased and displayed in their tens of thousands. No one could think of a human being, let alone an animal, who had received quite such an avalanche of adoration from being a victim of malice. Perhaps no horse had been thus treated since Caligula appointed his beloved Incitatus priest and consul, or the Emperor Lucius Verus's Celer was stalled in the Imperial palace, decked in Royal purple and worshipped by the Romans.

Sefton and Trooper Pedersen were sent to a fête at Chelsea Barracks to help raise money for the Sailors, Soldiers and Air Force Association. They drew the crowds as no other feature in the world could have done. 'Yes, thank you, he's enjoyed the limelight,' Pedersen told a newspaperman; 'he always does, but I'm afraid the limelight might spoil him!' They appeared on television, too, twice on the *Blue Peter* programme, to the delight of millions of children. That was not Sefton's debut in films: he had played a part in *Goodbye, Mr Chips*, long before he was a name to be conjured with.

Undergoing X-ray by the Royal Army Veterinary Corps. (Press Association)

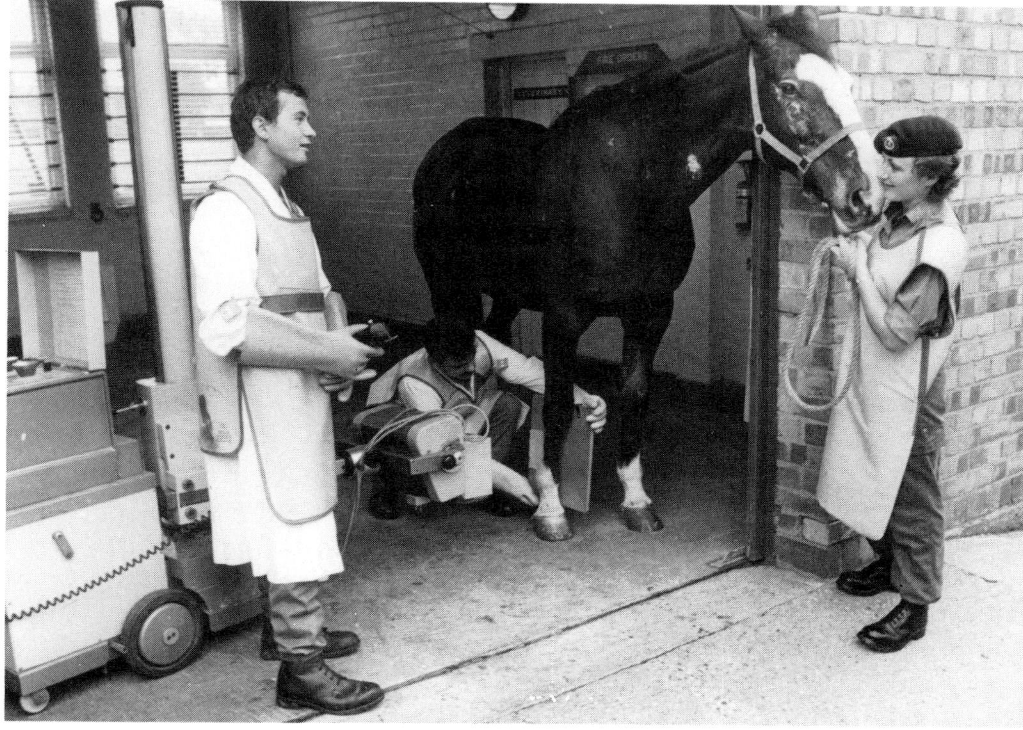

On the grass at Melton Mowbray with Corporal Islay Forbes. 'He knew exactly what was wanted of him,' she said, 'in the stable and out.' (Daily Express)

'Sefton ashtrays, Sefton medallions and Sefton pendants were purchased in their tens of thousands.'

By September his success was such that the director of the Horse of the Year Show, Mr John Stevens, who was direly short of bookings that year and earnestly seeking some sensation that might pull in the crowds and balance the books for him, applied to the Household Cavalry for Sefton to star as 'The Horse of the Year'. Sanction was granted for him to appear on the first evening, as the culminating turn of the Household Cavalry's Musical Ride.

The Ride's theme that year was *A Cavalry Kaleidoscope*, a historical pageant of Britain's mounted troops, the Ride being performed in period uniforms of seven regiments: the Royal Horse Guards in the 17th century; the 17th Dragoons in the 18th century; The Life Guards, the 11th Hussars and the 17th Lancers in the 19th century; and the 1st Royal Dragoons between the Wars. With the IRA iniquity very fresh in everyone's memory, the commentator reminded the audience of the valorous and noble character of the war-horse; of his patience and endurance; of his lack of complaint or self-pity in adversity; of the bond of affection between him and his trooper; and of the inestimable service and sacrifice given and made by him in the service of Britain's Kings and Queens down the ages.

At the end of the performance the cavalrymen charged up the arena to halt dramatically in front of the Royal Box. The lights were then turned off, and the Ride divided and single filed down the long sides of the great arena, and so out of the doors at the opposite end. Next a spotlight was beamed on the entrance, and in came Sefton, led by Pedersen. When the applause began the old hero responded with a buck and a whinny of joy – beautifully timed! – and

'Sefton and Trooper Pedersen were sent to a fête at Chelsea Barracks to raise money for SSAFA. They drew the crowds as no other feature in the world could have done.' (Daily Express)

the cheering eddied out to a prolonged and colossal roar. Nothing like it had ever before been heard at Wembley. Notwithstanding the dim lights you could see pocket handkerchiefs spreading through the stands like the start of snow on hillsides. The sobbing was contagious and quite unashamed. The scene was witnessed by millions of others on television sets. Sefton was England's darling and England was not too coy to show it.

Applications for seats for the remainder of the week's performances came flooding in. Sefton's presence not only altered the tone and spirit of the Show, but put the Show in the black. Would the Household Cavalry allow him to attend every matinee and every evening in the same solo style? Yes, they would. The Sefton adoration, the Sefton cult, went to the verge of worship when, on the last evening, he stood as the centrepiece of the Grand Finale, surrounded by the lesser stars of the Show, topnotchers of every shape and size, showjumpers and heavy horses, Pony Club competitors and Police horses, show hacks and heavyweight cobs, horses bearing disabled riders and horses bearing steeplechase jockeys, dressage horses, midgets harnessed for driving and, most important of all, his fellow-blacks in the Musical Ride from Knightsbridge. Never had Ronald Duncan's panegyric – written a decade before expressly in honour of the Horse of the Year Show – seemed more appropriate:

> This Cavalcade of Grace now stands, it speaks in silence. Its story is the story of this land.
>
> Where, in this wide world, can man find nobility without pride, friendship without envy or beauty without vanity? Here, where grace is laced with muscle, and strength by gentleness confined.
>
> He serves without servility; he has fought without enmity. There is nothing so powerful, nothing less violent; there is nothing so quick, nothing so patient.
>
> England's past has been borne on his back. All our history is his industry: we are his heirs, he our inheritance.
>
> Ladies and Gentlemen: THE HORSE!

Spectators searched through watered eyes for Sefton's scars. The powerful spotlights could not pick out a single sign of them on that glossy, ebony body. He was as impeccable, as smart, as glowing with health, as he had been when he left the barrack-gate, destined for a Whitehall box, at 10.35 am on July the 20th. It seemed like a miracle.

'He was England's darling and England was not too coy to show it.' (Leslie Lane)

Epilogue

Sefton's model of character and courage has been an inspiration to millions. Here is one particularly moving case. A ten-year-old votary of horses, a Sussex girl called Victoria Hart, was one of the host who sent him get-well cards. Suffering from cancer she had a leg amputated at about that time, and her parents feared for her life. She told them that Sefton's example of how to pull through gave her the will to recover, too. When her aunt in Carlisle heard of it, she wrote to the Household Cavalry begging them to allow her niece to see the horse. They promptly dispatched a greetings card – from Sefton to his fan – and an invitation to come and meet him.

In November Victoria not only said how-do-you-do to her hero, and gave him the carrot she had bought and the drawing she had made of him, but, in turn, she received a guided tour of the barracks. Victoria's morale soared.

People who heard of that, and of other incidents connected with the wounded cavalry horses, wrote passionately to the papers: it was only 'yellow-bellied, hysterical, fantasy-loving humans', they insisted, who fussed over their ailments. Animals were 'philosophical, stoical, intrepid, the most worthy examples for mankind to emulate, if only mankind would recognise it...'

Many thousands of people besides Victoria Hart took a close interest in Sefton's future career, and the press responded. He could scarcely turn in his stall without the world knowing it! Would he be retired? the world wanted to know. Not he! Soon after the adulation of the Horse of the Year Show he was going on Guard again.

People who are aware what acute memories horses possess, particularly in the association of places and incidents, vowed that those that were struck on July the 20th would never again be persuaded to pass the fatal spot. It is a marvellous reflection on the faith which Household Cavalry horses have in their riders that none of them has jibbed. Not only that, but, on reaching the point on the South Carriageway, a new gesture, a new sound was made. Every morning since July 21st, 1982, as the soldiers of the Queen's Life Guard pass the place where the outrage occurred, they bring their swords from the 'shoulder' to the 'carry' in tribute to their lost comrades and horses. In its modest way this has come to be regarded as one of the most moving of London's rituals.

Early November found Sefton going at a spanking trot on the State Opening of Parliament, and the nation cheered again. How about the 1983 Musical Ride? The Riding Master was keen to have him, but his tendons were proving too much of a hazard for a strenuous part in it. So a compromise

(left): *Victoria Hart (aged 10) with Sefton and Trooper Pedersen. 'Sefton's example of how to pull through gave her the will to recover.' (Mike Roberts)*

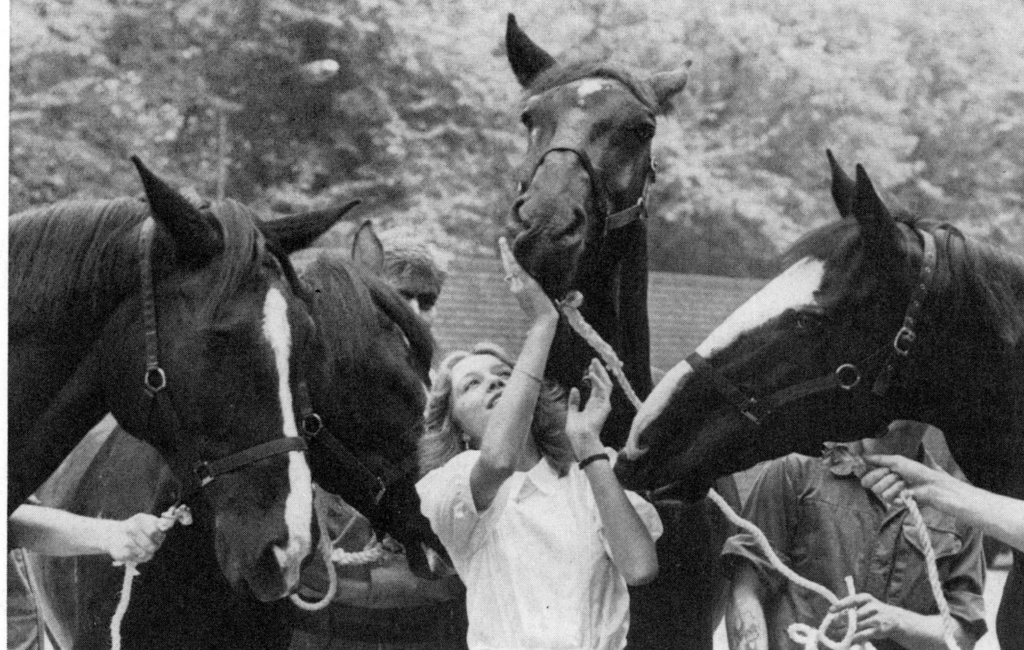

16-year-old Alison Slaughter with some of the horses that were injured. Left to right: Zany, Eclipse, Copenhagen and Sefton. (Press Association)

'Would he be retired?' the world wanted to know. 'Not he!' (Daily Express)

was made: a farrier, in full dress, carrying the axe of his office, was allotted Sefton, with the role of herald or marker. Now retained purely for ceremonial purposes, the axe was used, in the old days, in battle to remove a foot from dead horses, so that from the branded numbers, records could be kept of lost horses. The spike on the opposite side to the blade was used to put irrevocably wounded horses out of their misery.

20-year-old Sefton carrying a Farrier Corporal in his 1983 Musical Ride role. Lieutenant-Colonel and Riding Master Jackson stands by. Besides Corporal-Major McGregor, Colonel Jackson is the only one who has known Sefton since the beginning of his Army career. (Mike Roberts)

Sefton's understanding and physical prowess, his facility as a ceremonial and sporting horse, his whole style, spring from his innate and unique character, coupled with his environment and education as a Household Cavalry horse – starting with the rapport, the mutual trust, that arose between him and his trainer, Trooper McGregor, going on with the endeavours of those who brought him to great achievement in the Army of the Rhine, and continuing with the pomp and ceremony of Royal Britain, all the swagger of which he clearly cherishes for its own sake.

If people could go to the nub of what they really feel about Sefton, of what it is, in him, that they love, they might confess it to be his heart-and-soul generosity. Along with all the horses at Hyde Park Barracks, everything that he possesses he has given – in return for the ultimate in kindness, security and the job he relishes – to the Household Cavalry, and so by implication to his Colonel-in-Chief, the Queen, and all those of her subjects (and visitors to Britain, too) who are ready to respond to the magnificent performances that he and his friends, equine and human, have to offer.

Changing sentries. Sefton comes in from behind with the new relief.

'Soon after the adulation of the Horse of the Year Show he was going on Guard again.' Sefton is in the second half-section from the front, nearest the camera. (Mike Roberts)

Index

Anne, HRH Princess 98

Bandit (troop horse) 100
Batey, Corporal-Major R. (late Life Guards) 6, 64, 65, 100
Beaufort, Duke of (Master of the Horse) 27, 31
Booth-Jones, Major C.V. (late Royal Horse Guards) 57
Bonaparte, Napoleon 47
Boyd, Trooper (Blues and Royals) 54
Bright, Corporal-Major R. (Blues and Royals) 84, 88, 91, 98
Broughton, Major Hon. A.H.G. (late Blues and Royals) 54

Carding, Veterinary-Major N.H. (RAVC/Blues and Royals) 6, 92, 98, 99
Carr-Ellison, Major J.McM. (Blues and Royals) 6
Catherine of Braganza, Queen 45
Cedric (troop horse) 91
Celer (Roman horse) 100
Charles II, King 13, 28, 36, 45, 75
Copenhagen (troop horse) 91, 100, 107
Cuneo, Terence (artist) 100

Daly, Lieut D.R.A. (Blues and Royals) 84, 87, 88, 91, 98
Davis, Police Constable 97
De Ritter, Major A.P. (Life Guards) 75
Dickens, Lance-Corporal (Blues and Royals) 82
Duncan, Ronald (poet) 104

Echo (Police horse) 91
Eclipse (troop horse) 87, 100, 107
Eclipse (Police horse) 91, 94
Edinburgh, HRH Prince Philip, Duke of 22, 31, 73, 96, 98
Epaulette (troop horse) 91

Falcon (Officer's charger) 84, 91
Ferguson, Major R.I. (late Life Guards) 22
Forbes, Corporal I. (WRAC) 6, 8, 100, 101
Foxhunter (showjumper) 25
Frearson, Mr C.W. (Household Cavalry Museum) 6

Gauntlet (Trumpeter's horse) 93
George III, King 36
Gilbart-Denham, Major S.V. (Life Guards) 6

Hadden-Patton, Capt N. (Blues and Royals) 76
Hardy, Lt-Col Sir R. (late Life Guards) 27
Hart, Miss Victoria 105, 106
Haworth-Booth, Major C.N. (late Life Gaurds) 6, 58, 61—4
Henry VIII, King 35
Higgins (troop horse) 82
Hugh-Smith, Lt-Col H.O. (Blues and Royals) 22, 27

Incitatus (Roman horse) 100

Jackson, Lt-Col and Riding Master A. (Life Guards) 6, 67, 72, 79, 105, 109

Kent, William (architect) 36, 37

Lawson, Mr P.B. (Regimental Corporal Major) 84, 91
Laycock, Major J. (late RAVC)17, 18
Loyd, Major W.T.V. (late Life Guards) 6

Mary II, Queen 35

Monmouth, James, Duke of (Life Guards) 38
Morgan-Jones, Col K.R. (RAVC) 8
Mountbatten, Admiral of the Fleet, Earl, of Burma (Life Guards) 31, 38, 66

McGlade, Trooper (Life Guards) 64
McGregor, Corporal-Major D. (Blues and Royals) 6, 21, 22, 24, 25–7, 29–32, 41, 42, 108, 109
McNab, Mrs E. (Guards Magazine) 6

Nevill, Lord Rupert (late Life Guards) 98

Oates, Titus (dissident) 38
O'Flaherty, Corporal-of-Horse (Life Guards) 92
Ogilvie, Will H. (poet) 95

Parker-Bowles, Lt-Col A.H. (Blues and Royals) 6, 59, 76, 89, 92, 98
Pedersen, Trooper M. (Blues and Royals) 6, 80, 82, 83, 90, 92, 100, 102, 103, 106, 111
Philips, Trooper A. (Blues and Royals) 80, 82
Pitt, Corporal-of-Horse J. (Blues and Royals) 88

Quo Minus (troop horse) 100

Ringlet (troop horse) 100
Rochester (troop horse) 91
Roffey, Major P.A. (RAVC) 6

Salamander (troop horse) 100
Schofield, Major H.W. (late RAPC Guards Magazine) 6
Scott, Capt H. (Life Guards) 84
Sefton, Major the Earl of (Royal Horse Guards) 23
Slaughter, Miss Alison 107
Smith, Farrier-Major B. (Blues and Royals) 6, 97, 98
Spence, Sir Basil (architect) 19
Spurrey, Lt-Col J. (RAVC) 16
Stamford, Corporal-of-Horse (late Blues and Royals) 39, 67
Stevens, Mr John (Horse of the Year Show) 6, 102
Stroller (showjumper) 25
Sullivan, Trumpeter S. (Blues and Royals) 93

Templer, Field-Marshal Sir Gerald (Blues and Royals) 31, 38, 66
Thatcher, Mrs Denis 99
Tipper, Trooper (Blues and Royals) 91
Tweedie, Major G.H. (Blues and Royals) 59

Victoria, Queen 38, 66, 67, 75

Wales, HRH the Prince of 73, 75, 76
Wales, HRH the Princess of 75, 76
Walker-Okeover, Capt P.R.L. (Blues and Royals) 73
Waterford (troop horse) 87, 91
Wexford (troop horse) 54
Whitaker, Mr James (Daily Star) 89–91
White-Spunner, Capt B.W.B. (Blues and Royals) 6
Wilkinson, Capt R.C. (Blues and Royals) 56, 58–61
Wilkinson, Mrs R.C. 6
William III, King 35

Young, Lance-Corporal (Blues and Royals) 91
Yeastvite (troop horse) 91

Zara (troop horse) 91
Zany (troop horse) 100, 107